NORWICH AT WAR

This German aerial photograph of Norwich is dated January 1941. Thorpe railway station is at the left-hand side, nearly halfway down; Bishop Bridge is in the top left-hand corner. Thorpe St Andrew is top right, and Trowse bottom right.

Primary targets for bombers included factories, coalyards and power stations, and these are marked in red; the River Yare would have been the key feature looked for by German air crews when they were trying to get their bearings.

The Baedeker raids on cities like Norwich and Exeter extended the bombers' objectives to historic cities; these raids in April 1942 were the worst that Norwich was to experience.

GB 50 99 b c
Nur für den Dienstgebrauch

Bild Nr. 575 L/131

Aufnahme vom 3. 9. 39

Norwich
Hauptkraftwerk Thorpe

Länge (ostw. Greenw.): 1° 19' 20"   Nördl. Breite: 52° 37' 15"

Mißweisung: — 9° 56' (Mitte 1940)   Zielhöhe über NN 15 m

Maßstab etwa 1 : 10 000

Genst. 5. Abt.   Januar 1941

Karte 1 : 100 000
GB/E Bl. 19

1. Kraftzentrale (Kessel-, Maschinen- und Schalthaus)
2. Kohlenförderanlage
3. Kohlenhalde
4. Transformatorenfreiluftanlage

NORWICH AT WAR

THIRD EDITION

Joan Banger

POPPYLAND PUBLISHING

To my late father, Percy Scott (Scottie), without whose personal records this book could not have been written.

© 1974, 1989, 2002 Joan Banger
First published 1974
Second edition 1989
This edition published 2003 by Poppyland Publishing, 4 Alfred Road, Cromer, NR27 9AN
ISBN 0 946148 61 9

Designed by Watermark, Cromer NR27 9HL
Printed by Printing Services (Norwich) Ltd

An unrecorded house on an unrecorded steet, when Norwich was at War

Acknowledgements

Gratitude is expressed to many Norwich people who searched their records and memories and gave both for use in the preparation of the first and subsequent editions of this book. In particular, the following people and organizations: F J Bailey, Mrs Baldry, M Banger, Olive Bush, Mr Damsell, Bert Galey, Eddie Gates, P Gooch, Ruth Hardy, V E Harrison, A Howlett, Mrs Jackson, W G Kemp, E J Read, E F Scales, F Steward, J Ward, E S West, A B Whittingham, Mr Paul of Boulton and Paul, Eric Hinde of Bonds, Guy Greene of Watney Mann (East Anglia), Norwich Union Publicity Dept, Colman's Publicity Dept, Messrs Barnards. I would also like to thank Mr Jenner and the staff of Eastern Counties Newspapers and Mr Philip Hepworth, the Norwich City Librarian and his staff, for all their help. Lastly I would like to thank my husband for his endless help and tolerance. Special thanks are offered to Mrs Valerie Watts for the use of her father's leaflets for the 2002 edition.

The majority of the photographs that appear in this book have been generously supplied by Eastern Counties Newspapers Ltd. There are a number of other pictures reproduced by kind permission of the following people and organizations: Norwich Corporation, W G Kemp, George Swain, Messrs Bonds, Mr Dodger, C R Temple.

The principal documentary sources consulted were City of Norwich Civil Defence Files, Norwich Corporation Files, Norfolk and Norwich Record Office, Eastern Counties Newspapers, German Federal Republic Militärarchiv.

Sandbags are moved into position at City Hall.

Contents

Preface

The words of the introduction for the first edition of this book were written in 1974. Since then it has been in constant demand, though it has been out of print for some time. The opportunity was taken in the 1989 edition to include 50 extra photographs which were omitted from that first edition, but which serve to illustrate further the damage Norwich suffered. More new pictures, some now in colour, have been added for the 2002 edition. Sixty years on from the Norwich blitz, we have fewer people with direct memories of those frightening nights, but a continuing demand for information on Norwich's wartime years.

Apart from a few minor typographical errors which have been corrected, the bulk of the text of the 1974 edition is unaltered. The care of Joan Banger's research has stood the test of time and will continue to form the principal record of 'Norwich at War'.

As one of the main demands for a new edition of the book comes from schools, Poppyland Publishing has set up special web pages to support this title. Visit *www.poppyland.co.uk* and click on the 'Support' button for information.

Introduction

Every book has its origin somewhere. This book began life in a dustbin. When a man dies, and his personal effects are sorted, papers relating to a war that took place many years previously at first glance seem unimportant and so, along with the usual mass of miscellaneous papers, they are consigned to the dustbin for burning.

Luckily in this case, before the match was lit it was noticed that certain folders were of an official looking nature and they were retrieved. On examination the folders were found to contain records and material relating to the bombing of Norwich during the period 1940–1943.

Because of my personal memories of those days I found them of great interest, but incomplete, and so began a three year period of research as I endeavoured to fill the many gaps. At first material was hard to come by and in my search I made rather a pest of myself, but slowly, with patience and probing, more and more relevant documents appeared. Nevertheless if your personal experiences are not recorded here or the street in which you lived was bombed and is not accounted for in these pages you must forgive me for the mass of this book was compiled from official records and in a great many cases information is missing or lost for ever. In fact, the one clear lesson research has taught me is the importance of preserving records.

Norwich was selected as a target because of its 'beauty and unique historic interest' – not my words but those spoken by the enemy in 1942. Maybe that is why Norwich, in 1940, had the unenviable distinction of being the first place of any size to be bombed and also the first city to be mentioned by name in the official records.

JRB

The Government issued a series of leaflets advising the population what to do in various eventualities.

Prelude to War

Norwich Monday 3 October 1938

The King's words, on this October day in 1938, were being read with relief and delight by the citizens of Norwich. His Majesty had said: 'The time of anxiety is past, we have been able today to offer our thanks to the Almighty for His mercy in sparing us the horror of war.'

The 'horror of war' had very much preoccupied the people of Norwich. In May of this year an Air Raid Precautions officer had been appointed to the City. Throughout the year there had been many appeals for volunteers to join the ARP. Some 3,500 people were needed for the 250 Air Raid Posts planned. A Report Centre was to be built which would need to be staffed, and dispatch messengers were also wanted. Volunteers were also needed to form Decontamination Squads and it was the thought of gas attack that really put fear into people's minds. They remembered the tales of gas attacks during the First World War, and the descriptions of choking lungs and blistering skins. But now it seemed the threat of war that had loomed so appallingly near was receding. And the people rejoiced.

The feeling of relief was short-lived. In the weeks that followed the newspapers still asked for volunteers. People at first closed their minds to such things. It was only human that once the immediate peril had disappeared such grim preparations should be forgotten. The response to these appeals was exceedingly disappointing but over the weeks of threatened war a nucleus had been born, committees had been formed, and ideas put forward. It was suggested that churches could be used as first aid posts. It was debated whether the trenches in Chapel Field Gardens ought to be filled in or remain. There was talk of the advisability of purchasing eight

YOUR GAS MASK

How to keep it
and How to Use it

MASKING YOUR
WINDOWS

PUBLIC INFORMATION
LEAFLET   NO. 2

Read this and
keep it carefully.
You may need it.

Issued from the Lord Privy Seal's Office July, 1939

AIR RAID PRECAUTIONS
HANDBOOK No. 1
(2nd Edition)

PERSONAL PROTECTION
AGAINST GAS

HIS MAJESTY

The public was advised on many aspects of life during wartime through various leaflets and booklets. The perils of gas and air warfare had become apparent in the 1930s and the booklets were ready when required.

SOME THINGS YOU
SHOULD KNOW IF
WAR SHOULD COME

PUBLIC INFORMATION
LEAFLET   NO. 1

Read this and
keep it carefully.
You may need it.

Issued from the Lord Privy Seal's Office July, 1939

YOUR FOOD IN
WAR-TIME

PUBLIC INFORMATION
LEAFLET   NO. 4

Read this and
keep it carefully.
You may need it.

Issued from the Lord Privy Seal's Office July, 1939

AIR RAID PRECAUTIONS
HANDBOOK No. 2
(1st Edition)

ANTI-GAS PRECAUTIONS AND
FIRST AID FOR AIR RAID
CASUALTIES

LONDON
HIS MAJESTY'S STATIONERY OFFICE
1935
Price 6d. Net

Corporation buses for conversion into ambulances; they could be bought for £25 each, which included free storage for six months, and conversion would cost a further £2–1s.

The seeds had been sown.

In October Norwich was to have a Civic Week and this rather over-shadowed Air Raid Precautions, although they were to be much in evidence. There was to be an Air Display at Mousehold Aerodrome. The Auxiliary Firemen were to give a fire-fighting display and there was to be a torchlight procession by members of the various voluntary organisations who were to walk with electric torches, together with many tableaux from City shops and clubs. The tensions of the year were broken as tens of thousands of the City's people turned out to cheer.

On the Saturday of the Civic Week festivities there was to be a grand finale. The King and Queen were coming to open the newly built City Hall. So the year of 1938 went on.

Professor Haldane, speaking at a meeting in the City, was to strike a note of fear when he said that Norwich was in a particularly exposed position to air attacks as it was the furthest east of any of the great cities of England. The year was to end with a confused populace, attending meetings on peace and listening to air raid sirens being tested. As snow fell bringing the traffic to a standstill, the temperature dropped to 29.1 degrees Fahrenheit and the year ended.

1939

The New Year came in with people still completely confused. The newspapers announced that Norwich would not be evacuated in the event of air raids; how this would have been done anyway was never made clear. The alarm siren system was designed to give a minimum of eight minutes grace for the populace to take cover.

By February the hard-working committees had decided that the trenches dug during the previous year's crisis periods should be deepened and permanently maintained, with shrubs planted on top of them.

In March the Prime Minister, Neville Chamberlain, denounced Adolf Hitler as a breaker of his word.

April brought some relief in the form of London's long-running musical *Me and My Girl* being performed at the Theatre Royal, and the streets of Norwich rang with the strains of 'The Lambeth Walk' as people danced

A page from within the booklet illustrated on page 8.

FITTING RESPIRATORS

In fitting a Respirator, attention must be given to the wearer's (a) **Protection** ; (b) **Comfort** ; and (c) **Efficiency** whilst working or moving about.

Fitting the Civilian Respirator. (Fig. 14.)

With the Respirator held up by the webbing-straps and with the straps well open, the wearer thrusts foward his chin, the straps are drawn over the head, and are adjusted through the iron buckle at the back of the head.

Care must be taken to see that the rubber edges of the facepiece are not turned in, that the straps are not twisted, that the buckle is centred on the back of the head, that the facepiece is straight on the face with the two side-straps level over the ears, and that the rubber of the facepiece fits tightly under the chin.

The facepiece must not fit too tightly against the wearer's eyebrows ; and the wearer's eyes should appear *near the middle* of the transparent window. **If the eyes are too high, the facepiece is too small** : if too low, **the facepiece is too large.**

In general, men require the large size, women the medium size, and children the small size.

If the Respirator is gastight, the wearer will find difficulty in breathing in when **a sheet of cardboard is held tightly over the bottom end of the container.** When the correct fit is ascertained, the position of the buckle on the straps is marked by a pencil line and the straps are secured with the safety pins provided so that no further adjustment for the wearer will be required to make the Respirator ready for use.

Spectacles cannot safely be worn under the Respirator.

To REMOVE THE CIVILIAN RESPIRATOR : Holding the container in the left hand, insert the thumb of the right under the buckle at the back of the head and pull the buckle forward over the top of the head so that the Respirator is lowered downwards from the face.

Fig. 14.
Fitting Civilian Respirator

(a) Front view holding headstraps ; (b) Side view with chin well out, before putting on ; (c) Testing for gastightness with cardboard ; (d) Removing Respirator.

24

and sang this popular song. It must have been a very welcome diversion.

Later in the month the Prime Minister announced conscription for all young men aged 20 and 21 and by this time, although still desperately trying to convince themselves that war was not inevitable, doubt was creeping into people's minds.

The beginning of May, and the City's air raid trenches were walled with concrete and provided with airlocks to make them gas-proof. By the end of the month a more ambitious scheme was put forward by the ARP Committee. This was to provide deep public shelters by cutting tunnels into the chalk ridges on which the city stands. Chalk workings already existed off Newmarket Road near Eaton Hill and at Thompson's factory in Rosary Road and these could be used. The castle mound was also considered as a possible tunnelling site. Much time and thought were given to these projects but the inevitable snags were found and the foremost of these was cost. Estimates for these schemes were as follows:

86,000 persons at £10–10s per head.	
Tunnelling in chalk bank to 60 feet	£903,000
4,000 persons at £8 per head.	
Tunnelling in waterlogged ground to 60 feet	£32,000
61,000 persons at £20 per head	
in the Castle Mound	£1,200,000
2,500 persons at £18 per head	
at the Cattle Market	£45,000
4,000 persons at £13-10s per head	£54,000
14,000 school children at £15 per head	£210,000
171,500	**£2,444,000**

The Corporation, confronted by this estimate, must have been shocked and the scheme was never to mature. The ARP Committee now spoke of protecting a percentage of the population. Norwich, they felt, needed 26,000 Anderson shelters as a supplement to the trenches and surface shelters. By now the adult population had been issued with gas masks and in July it was time to attend to the needs of our most junior citizens. There were demonstrations of 'How to use a Baby's Gas-Mask'. Children from two to four and a half years had a small child's respirator, and those aged from four and a half to five years were issued with a small sized civilian mask. The liability of young children attempting to remove respirators if

CIVILIAN RESPIRATOR

REMOVING THE CIVILIAN RESPIRATOR   CIVILIAN DUTY RESPIRATOR

ADJUSTING THE CIVILIAN RESPIRATOR

CIVILIAN ANTI-GAS SCHOOL

VENTILATED GAS-PROOF SHELTER   RESPIRATOR SUPPLY DEPOT   TRAINEES PASSING THROUGH MOBILE GAS VAN

A GARDEN DUG-OUT

A FRENCH GAS-PROOF BALLOON SHELTER

SERVICE RESPIRATOR, VALVE & CONTAINER

they became tired of wearing them was recognized and it was thought that some form of restraint might be necessary to control their arms. This must have been a sobering thought. The small baby a few months old was the greatest problem. The gas mask was a large helmet consisting of a padded hood with a window surrounded by a metal frame. It was fitted with an adjustable tailpiece turned up at the end to form a seat and prevent the child from slipping out of the head. Air was supplied by pumping a bellows through a filter – a slow steady rate of pumping was required. The young mothers of Norwich were horrified as the baby used in the demonstration screamed as it was placed in the respirator.

Although gas was not used in bombing raids, many feared that it would be, and all the population was issued with gas masks.

The end of the month, and children evacuated from London arrived in Norwich; one weekend five train-loads arrived on the Saturday and a further seven on Sunday. On the Cattle Market shelters for 3,500 were being hurriedly dug. These were to be of the trench type and concrete lined.

One of the popular methods of educating people in what they should do in an air raid was through cigarette cards. These could be collected and kept in albums as shown on page 10.

In the City preparations for war gained momentum. Facts had to be faced at last. As September approached the days of vain hopes were over. And then on 3 September at 11am came Chamberlain's now famous announcement that 'a state of war exists . . .'

People were stunned and apprehensive about what would happen next. Imagination ran riot. But nothing did happen, even though at 2.42am that night the air raid siren sent people rushing to the shelters where they remained, listening intently for aircraft engines, for 37 minutes before they were released by the sound of the All Clear. They emerged having experienced the first of the many 'false alarms' that were to follow during the coming months. But in these many fruitless journeys to the shelters the foundation of a new relationship among neighbours was born, a companionship of shared fears, where people became less selfish, helped with each other's children or shared a flask of tea. People were thrown together in the sort of close proximity that is usually so alien to the Norfolk character.

During the next ten months running to the shelter became a game that quickly lost its charm and the wailing note of the Alert gradually became largely ignored. It was not until July of the following year that the rules of this game were changed and the citizens found that trouble could come unheralded by any siren . . .

The Raids

Raid 1

9 July 1940 (Tuesday) No Alert

It was five o'clock on a warm summer afternoon and from high in the sky the dull throb of aircraft engines could be heard. No air raid siren had been sounded. There was no cause for alarm.

The employees of Barnards' factory at Mousehold saw two aircraft approaching from the north-east, flying at about 600 feet. As they made out the black markings in the shape of crosses on the wings they flung themselves to the ground. The explosions that followed were curiously light, sharp cracks and certainly not the heavy and prolonged reverberations everybody had been expecting. The most frightening features were the vibrating walls, the sound of breaking glass, and the noise of splinters, stones and earth hitting walls and falling on roofs. The raid was all over in six long seconds.

There were three casualties. Harry Leonard Dye, a packer, and Arthur Shreeves, a driver, were working by the loading dock and both received fatal injuries. Ronald Green, the dispatch foreman, was the third casualty. He threw himself to the ground some 20 yards from where the bomb exploded but his only injury was a damaged toe that was later amputated. Arthur Adams of the dispatch office had a most remarkable escape when a bullet or bomb splinter went through his trouser leg while others pierced the walls on either side of him. This factory site, made up of hangars and outbuildings, was hit by 12 high-explosive 250 kg bombs. Three unexploded bombs were also dropped. One of the aircraft was seen to bank

THE KING'S QUOTATION

Daily Press

Telegrams: "Press, Norwich."

WEDNESDAY, DECEMBER 27, 1939 — THREE HALF-PENCE

…ements

…ANT

…EPERS

…eek in January …ooke; three in … outings.—Box (D27

…es according to …ottage Hospital.

…er 40), wtd. nr. …n sitting-room …one with child) …land, Norwich.

…HOUSE-

…Norwich, £36. …mf. post. …s' Green, N'ch.

…LLERYMAIDS

… first week in …ary: not under …and references. …, Norfolk.

HOUSES, SHOPS, &c., WANTED

WANTED. HIRE LIVING VAN at once for two men, near Norwich.—S. H. Witham, Erpingham Norwich. 'Phone: Hanworth 251. (D29

COUNTRY HOUSES AND PROPERTIES FOR SALE OR TO LET

FAKENHAM, 2¼ miles.—Excellent BUNGALOW, all modern conveniences, elec., water, bath, h. and c., hal., 5 rooms, garage, garden, summer house; easy station, snip, freehold £600, possession rates covered.—G. Trollope, Watton. (D28

SHIPDHAM.—PAIR Brick-Tile COTTAGES; sheds, gardens; one vacant with stable, paddock, small field; price £250.—Trollope, Watton. (D28

WEST NORFOLK.—Capital 6-Roomed HOUSE, hall, kitchen, garage, washhouse, sheds, garden, orchard; vacant; £500.—G. Trollope, Watton. (D28

WANTED

WANTED TO RENT between Hunstanton and Cromer, within easy distance of sea, UNFURNISHED SMALL COUNTRY COTTAGE, 2 or 3 bedrooms, indoor sanitation essential.—Tremaine, 47 North Brink, Wisbech.

FARMS, LAND, &c., FOR SALE OR TO LET

334-ACRE LINCOLNSHRE FARM to Let, near village and station; large grass area (about 200 acres) with house and farm buildings; entry 6th April next low rent.—Full particulars from the Country Gentlemen's …

AIR RAID PRECAUTIONS

BEAT the Black-out, Rechargeable HAND-LAMP, gives 100 hours' light, 14/-, made in accordance to regulations.—Fishers (opp. Theatre de Luxe Cinema), St. Andrew Street, Norwich.

TUITION

HOLIDAY TUITION IN WEAK SUBJECTS.—John A. Spence, 68, The Close, Norwich.

AGRICULTURAL

ALLIS CHALMERS TRACTORS ready for immediate delivery to you. Also a variety of RECONDITIONED TRACTORS. All makes of IMPLEMENTS.—Larkman & Sons, Besthorpe. 'Phone Attleborough 3147.

A. & W. CUSHION LTD., TIMBER MERCHANTS, BARN ROAD, NORWICH are open to purchase for cash Plantations of FIR TREES, also OAK, ASH, BEECH, WALNUT, and ENGLISH TREES of all description standing or felled. Full particulars to above address. Tel. 663.

CASKS FOR CIDER.—Fresh emptied WINE CASKS for Sale.—Prices, apply, R. Clarke, Cooper, 10, Ber Street, Norwich.

DAMP WHEAT and Smelly BARLEYS RECONDITIONED at the Old Maltings, Coltishall, 1/6 per coomb.—THOMAS W. COOKE, Aldborough, Norwich. 'Phone: Coltishall 6.

FAT PIGS, LONDONERS and FAT SOWS WANTED.—Apply G. Clarke, Wymondham. Telephone No. Wymondham 115.

FORDSON TRACTORS — Immediate delivery of New Machines on Spade Lugs or Pneumatics, prices from £155. Also reconditioned Tractors from £65.—J. J. Wright & …

A Devon Coxswain

WAR MEANS MORE PERILS FOR HIM TO FACE

The work of this vital Service must go on in War as well as in Peace.

In time of War it may be more difficult for you to contribute to the Life-Boat Service, but remember that these heroic men are working now in circumstances of far greater difficulty and danger.

Contributions, however small, are urgently required to maintain, this great national Institution.

Send us whatever you can afford.

ROYAL NATIONAL LIFE-BOAT INSTITUTION

The Eastern Daily Press still carried advertisements on its front page during the war years. This edition gives the period of the black-out at the top of the page. It also carries adverts specific to the war, such as 'Beat the Blackout' and an RNLI appeal ad reminding readers of the extra work for the lifeboats.

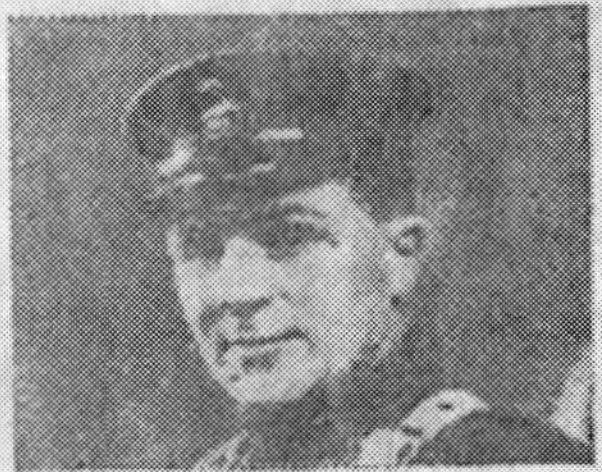

►►

This illustration of the Boulton and Paul factory is taken from a Luftwaffe (German air force) book of targets in Norwich. Such photos had often been copied from postcards or guidebooks.

►

Another useful publication for the householder.

away towards the centre of the City.

At Colman's Carrow Works people poured through the main gates – jostling, laughing, bicycle-bells ringing. As the aircraft suddenly appeared overhead groups of workers were pushing their bicycles up the steep slope of Carrow Hill. The aircraft banked a little and dived, then the sound of a whistling bomb rent the air. The older men, remembering the sound of falling bombs from the First World War, threw themselves to the ground, at the same time shouting to the women, 'Down!' The women and girls did not immediately abandon their bicycles – bicycles were precious in those days of low wages and represented the only alternative to long walks to work – and they did not throw themselves to the ground. The bomb crashed through the trees near the old tower at the top of Carrow Hill and exploded at ground level. The blast was not cushioned by the

bomb embedding itself in the ground, and it was later thought that during its passage through the trees the bomb's detonator had been triggered off, causing it to explode as it did. The brick wall in front of Tower Flats carried the scars for many years. When one looks at those gouged marks it is easy to visualize the scene of

This wall in Bracondale carried the scars of the first frightening raid for many years after the war.

horror on that hill the horror of blast, with its flying stones, earth, splinters, and broken glass. Several people were killed, some were seriously injured, and many suffered minor injuries.

There were to be many more bombs dropped on Norwich, but somehow, maybe because it was the first raid, or because of the innocence of the standing girls' upturned faces, this was to imprint on the minds of the survivors the full implications of modern warfare.

Boulton & Paul, the engineering firm who manufactured the famous Sopwith Camel and Snipe aircraft of the First World War, were now engaged in the construction of wooden fuselages for Oxford Trainer aircraft and the nose sections for Horsa gliders. It was the turn of their Riverside factory to feel the weight of the enemy next and four bombs scored direct hits. As explosion followed explosion, columns of smoke billowed into the sky. In the inferno that followed, ten lost their lives and many more were injured.

Nearby, bombs crashed on to the London & North Eastern Railway's locomotive sheds and hit railway lines, leaving them twisted and bent into weird upright shapes. In all, four bombs were dropped and there were fatal casualties and a number of seriously injured. There were several minor incidents: a bomb left a crater three feet deep on the roadway adjoining Carrow Bridge, making it unsafe; in King Street the roof and sides of a

It was bad enough sweets being rationed, without finding the sweet-shop had gone. (This one was in King Street.) Maybe you could still get a packet of ten cigarettes from the machine!

store under the backyard of the Kingsway public house collapsed and near number 262 a gas-main burst when a bomb fell at the back of the house. Another bomb fell near Allan Road damaging part of the old City wall.

So ended the first air raid on Norwich, with 27 of her citizens dead and many more injured. During those few brief moments people acquired new sensitivities, nostrils became attuned to the smell of air raids, compounded of burnt wood, soot, water, cloth, earth, and fear; and limbs and stomachs learnt new tensions. Although life went on it could never be the same.

Ironically, the Theatre de Luxe in St Andrew Street was showing Dust Be My Destiny, starring John Garfield and Priscilla Lane. To add to our troubles the Minister of Food chose this day to introduce tea rationing, but at least you could still buy an air raid shelter for £12–10s, complete and erected.

You had to remember to 'put up the blackout' by 9.44pm. Not that one could forget the blackout for long. At the slightest gleam the shout 'put that light out' would reverberate down the road, not always from the throat of a warden. After the first raid everyone became very conscious of the need for total blackout, a difficult thing to achieve in a city the size of Norwich. At night the tiny glow of a partly blacked-out torch was the only light you had to walk by and the headlamps of cars emitted two thin pencil-like beams of

light. People who had lived in the City all their lives found themselves lost and fumbling along walls to find some familiar feature.

Raid 2

19 July 1940 (Friday) No Alert

The sun was shining on this morning when at about 6am, without any Alert being sounded, a lone raider approached the City from the northeast. In two terraced cottages in Bull Close the Brooks family, at number 78, and the Steward family, at number 80, were sound asleep, as the aircraft's bomb doors opened.

At number 78 Alfred, Ronald, and Donald Brooks, aged ten, eight and four, were asleep in the Anderson shelter in the garden. Their elder brothers Geoffrey and Albert lay in the house in the middle bedroom and their parents were in the front bedroom. Mr and Mrs Brooks awoke to find a confusion of pictures and ornaments flying about. Jumping from their bed they found the whole room in ruins. Mrs Brooks later said: 'There was a terrific roar but I didn't realise at first it was our house that had been hit.' Mr and Mrs Brooks ran to the middle bedroom to find their two elder sons safe. They were staring at what once had been the doorway to the back bedroom but which was now an open void overlooking a pile of rubble. Mrs Brooks, calling to the three boys in the Anderson shelter, made her way downstairs. On reaching the bottom there was another crash and the staircase collapsed behind her. A ladder had to be found before Mr Brooks could join his wife to find the whole of his family alive and well.

Meanwhile, next door at number 80, Fred Steward was hurled from his bed by the blast. This no doubt saved his life as, with the impact of the explosion, his bed rolled up like a Venetian blind. The bomb had crashed into the kitchen, completely demolishing it together with the small bedroom above. The front of the house, although suffering great damage, remained intact thus saving the lives of his parents. Even the family budgerigar survived, although minus most of its feathers. The Stewards had lost most of their home but they had survived, and were thankful. And so too were the City Corporation, as Mr Steward senior was a member of a family with a tradition. In 1917 his father, Josh Steward had become Norwich Corporation's clock and watch repairer and he himself was now employed in maintaining clocks in the City Hall, the libraries, and the schools and churches. If that explosion had not blown Fred Steward junior from his bed, the 2,500 Corporation clocks would not have been for many years after the war attended, in the tradition of the family, by a Steward.

A lucky escape for the Steward family of Bull Close in Raid 2. Young Fred Steward is seen in the window.

Just behind these Bull Close cottages another bomb fell in Magdalen Close. This exploded near to a block of flats, cracking a wall. In Magdalen Street a garage lying behind the Cat and Fiddle public house received a direct hit. A number of cars were parked there, one of which was left with its nose pointing skywards to the demolished roof, while others were thrown about in disorder. In Botolph Street Hingles' furniture shop was completely destroyed by another bomb although the adjoining premises appeared to be little damaged. In St George Street Annison's fish shop was demolished and there was some slight damage to other property. Off Salhouse Road, Mousehold, the premises of the Norwich Aero Club, which had been unoccupied for several weeks, were burnt out and its covered tennis-courts destroyed.

When the dust settled on these new bomb sites people drifted by to look and to be thankful that, miraculously, there had been no serious injury. Only two people had been slightly wounded.

If people wished to forget what they had seen that morning Miss Mae West, the sex symbol of the day, was starring in My Little Chickadee down the road at the Odeon that evening. And if you had lost, or were worried about losing, your home at least you could look through the local newspaper and read: 'To Let, 18/- per week including rates, small detached House with garage, near Norwich.'

Raid 3

30 July 1940 (Tuesday) No Alert

Eleven days after Raid 2, again at six o'clock in the morning and with no Alert, a single Dornier 215 slowly circled the City and released its bombs over the River Wensum. Spouts of water rose high in the air as three bombs plunged into the water between Wire's farm in Hellesdon Road and Mile Cross Bridge.

Surrey Street Bus Station was the next target and here bombs fell on reinforced concrete and the blast was considerable. One double-decker bus was lifted off its front wheels and swung in ruins across the road; a second was totally wrecked – luckily both were unoccupied at the time. Also in Surrey Street more spouts of water were to be seen. They came from fractured water-mains as a crater 15 feet in diameter appeared in the roadway opposite number 29, then the Angel Hotel, and from the former water-works office on one side and the General Accident Assurance Office on the other. Houses on both sides of the street were damaged with windows shattering and ripped-off slates crashing to the pavement. Nevertheless, apart from superficial cuts, nobody was hurt.

In Ber Street, at number 68, a confectionery shop's double windows were blown out, raining sweets and broken glass on to the pavement. Mr and Mrs C W Parker, the owners, and their three children, who lived above the shop, had fortunate escapes. Another bomb fell in Ber Street, this time on wasteland at the rear of the George the Fourth public house; again there were no casualties. In Victoria Terrace, however, numbers 13 and 14 received a direct hit and numbers 12 and 15 were seriously damaged by blast. In this incident five people were hurt. Poor old Victoria Terrace; two more bombs crashed on to numbers 6 and 8 and caused serious damage to numbers 4, 5, 7 and 9. One can imagine the state of this small devastated terrace where ten people were killed or seriously injured.

In Compass Street number 3 received a direct hit and numbers 2, 4 and 5 were badly damaged. These houses were so old and in such poor condition that they pulled each other to the ground injuring seven people.

In Lorne Place, Argyle Street, the side of a house was hit, the point of impact lying close to numbers 1 and 2 – the only occupant, a lady, was killed. At 11 Argyle Street a 25 by five foot crater appeared in the soft soil at the rear of the house. Another bomb landed on soft soil near Read's Flour Mills in King Street, leaving a crater some seven feet deep. Colmans' Printing Department at the west end of Carrow Works was bombed

Somebody's home in Victoria Terrace.

and here the incident was dealt with by the company's own fire-fighting organization.

The bombs played a peculiar game of cricket across market gardens off Mansfield Lane where seven bombs were dropped about a cricket pitch length apart. One hoped that not too many fruit bushes had been damaged as the Ministry of Food had just announced a bonus issue of 2lb of sugar per ration book for jam-making.

At the Hippodrome they were showing *Strip Please* and you could count your money and choose your seat – 2s 6d, 1s 6d, 1s, or 6d. But at times like this it was hard to relax. You had to remember to immobilize your car whenever you left it, day or night, if you didn't want to be fined. The ARP were giving demonstrations of fire-fighting with a stirrup pump, which you really should

◀ Fire-fighting near St Andrew's Hall.

◀◀ This bus was an early casualty in Raid 3.

go to, and the newspapers were asking everybody to practise wearing their gas-masks for 15 minutes each week. A young nurse was fined 10s with 3s 6d costs for showing a light from a window after dark so you had to remember to put up the blackout curtains. Then there was the aluminium saucepan to be taken to the member of the WVS who had said that any kitchen pot or pan would do as long as it was made of aluminium and could eventually be converted into Spitfires. There was so much to think about in these war days, and if the programme at the Hippodrome was not your cup of tea then you could go to the Electric Theatre and see The Spirit of the People.

The Spitfire and Hurricane from local airfields became a common sight.

Raid 4

1 August 1940 (Thursday) No Alert

The first day of the month appeared to be passing peacefully, with no siren, and no having to rush down to the shelter. In Boulton & Paul's canteen at Riverside employees did not hear the Junkers 88 bomber swooping down to 400 feet as it flew in from the south-west of the City. Nor did they see the black and white cross on its fuselage. But maybe they heard the whistle of its bombs hurtling towards their factory and, more particularly, towards the paint shop which lay above them. The paint shop had been built in 1916 when wood was cheap and plentiful. The outside walls were heavily ornamented with mouldings and it was well stocked with varnishes and spirits, the perfect fuel for a major fire. When hit by two high explosive and two incendiary bombs it exploded in a sheet of fire. Nine people lost their lives: three women from the canteen, three more from the printing and stationery office, two men from the drawing office, and another from the joinery. It was only 22 days since they had experienced their first raid in which ten of their colleagues had died.

The aircraft's next target was Thorpe Station but only two bombs fell and one of these failed to explode. The plane, after dropping these bombs, made off in the direction of the coast but not before directing a parting burst of machine-gun fire towards the King Street, Prince of Wales Road and Thorpe Station area. Here several more people were killed. Many policemen sustained minor injuries for they, like members of the AFS and ARP wardens, always appeared on the scene with incredible speed. One of the casualties was 89 year old Mrs Randell, who was taken to hospital suffering from cuts. Flying glass and roof tiles caused most of the minor injuries.

The citizens of Norwich gave generously this week to the Sheriff's appeal for funds to buy one or more Spitfires. They must have felt it would be a grand addition to their war effort if a Spitfire could bear the name 'City of Norwich'.

In another branch of the City's war effort – salvage collection – we led the rest of the County. In a 24 week period the following was collected:

Paper	460 tons	£1,172
Metal	40 tons	176
Textiles	33 tons	461
Bottles, jars	1,540 gross	280
Bones	4 tons	10
Skins	56 dozen	4
total		**£2,103**

That evening you could see Fred MacMurray and Barbara Stanwyck in Remember that Night or perhaps you preferred to stay at home and listen to the wireless, possibly rented for 1s 11d a week.

Raid 5

10 August 1940 (Saturday) Alert 18.08 hours

At just past six o'clock in the evening anti-aircraft guns were heard from the east engaging enemy planes. The gunners must have done a good job as only three bombs were dropped on the City. One went through the roof of a large timber shed at Colmans' Carrow Works causing little damage and no fire, while the other two failed to make direct hits on buildings but their blast damaged the side of a storage shed roof. There was one slightly injured casualty.

This month at Norwich Magistrates' Court a Home Guard officer was fined 10s 6d and ordered to pay 5s 6d costs for permitting the glow of a cigarette to be visible in the street while an air-raid warning was in operation.

At the Odeon Theatre Deanna Durbin was appearing in the film It's a Date, and at the Theatre Royal that well-known entertainer Norman Long, the first comedian to broadcast in the old Savoy Hill days, was appearing in the show Yes That's Right, starring Claude Dampier.

The Norwich Milk Officer informed the citizens that dried milk was shortly to be made available. It would be issued in 20 oz containers, a normal week's supply.

Contributors to charity funds to buy aircraft were being shown the cost of different types of aircraft – Spitfire £6,000; Hurricane £4,500; Blenheim £17,000; Wellington £25,000; Sunderland £50,000.

Raid 6

20 August 1940 (Tuesday) No Alert

At about 3am, during an All Clear period, incendiary bombs were dropped, falling at random. Number 24 Supple Close received an incendiary in its backyard, some 20 feet from the house. This was quickly smothered with sand by an air raid warden. At 17 Brian Avenue a bomb just burnt itself out in the garden and another bounced off the roof of 8 Davey Place doing only slight damage. A cottage used for offices in Stamp Office Yard, St Andrew Street, suffered some damage to its upper room and roof, while at

the rear of 31 Surrey Street a small fire was quickly extinguished. It was a wise procedure to deal with these small incendiary-bomb fires swiftly as larger conflagrations could act as beacons for following aircraft, possibly loaded with high-explosive bombs, and although on this occasion no aircraft were to follow the initial attacker it was as well to be sure.

Incendiary bombs were best dealt with by throwing a sandbag over them; it did not extinguish the magnesium but it controlled it and reduced the heat making the situation manageable. The stirrup pump was a useful and inexpensive appliance for putting out fires in their early stages. It worked from a bucket and was used extensively by civilians and Civil Defence personnel. All householders were advised to have sandbags and water-buckets available and for emergencies the Corporation had built several 5,000 gallon water-tanks (see Appendix 10).

Anyone injured as a result of enemy action received help from the Assistance Board where immediate grants could be obtained by injured people who had temporarily lost their earning power. A married man was allowed £1-5s a week while in hospital and £1-13s a week when he came out and in addition he could claim 4s a week for each of his first two children and 3s a week for any further children. For an unmarried man the rates were 11s a week while in hospital and £1 per week when convalescent. A single woman was entitled to 9s 6d a week while in hospital and 18s a week when convalescent.

The British Red Cross, in conjunction with the Women's Institute, had organized depots containing

Lady Wardens can still smile!

second-hand clothing all over Norfolk, a service the populace prayed they would never need to take advantage of – in fact this could be the reason why a demonstration of fire-fighting given by the wardens of Post G5 this month drew a crowd of about a thousand people.

With the close of August the air war spread to other cities and on 7 September 1940 London received its first air raid.

Raid 7

18/19 September 1940 (Wednesday)
Alert 20.54 hours

Just four bombs were dropped in this raid, two incendiary oil bombs and two delayed-action high-explosive bombs – they fell 55 minutes after midnight. One of the delayed-action bombs fell on heathland at Long Valley, Mousehold, and exploded 12 hours later, while the two incendiaries, which also fell in Long Valley, caused only minor fires to heathland; in fact three very lucky escapes for Norwich. The second delayed-action bomb, a 1,000 pounder, made a crater in the pavement of

Removing a bomb from Theatre Street; on the right, Chief Warden V E Harrison looks on.

Theatre Street, by Church Street, damaging a gas-main and thus adding to the hazards facing the Bomb Disposal Squad. It certainly created great disruption in the City, as it was not removed until 24 September, with the whole area evacuated and notices posted restricting entrance. The unexploded bomb was a most unwelcome neighbour for the Arts Ballet Company who were performing at the Theatre Royal, having removed from London earlier than intended when the air raids there interrupted their work.

During this month of September the air-raid siren was sounded some 129 times with not a single day clear.

Raid 8

27 October 1940 (Sunday) Alert 17.45 hours

The dull drone of the raiders' engines was heard from the south-east and fierce anti-aircraft fire met them as they approached the City. One plane was seen to break off in a southerly direction hotly pursued by a Spitfire but three other aircraft carried on and reached the outskirts of Norwich. A bus shelter in Middleton Lane, Hellesdon, was machine-gunned, the bullets sweeping along Middleton Lane, Links Close, and Palmer Road. A bungalow in Orchard Close was demolished by a high-explosive bomb and several other homes had their roofs damaged. Three bombs, two of which failed to explode, hit Norwich Aero Club's field at Salhouse Road, Mousehold, and a fire in their hangar was quickly brought under control. In all these events there were no casualties reported.

The plantation on the west side of the hangars and the gardens of the adjoining War Memorial Cottages were hit by several delayed-action bombs which exploded the following day bringing down telephone wires and uprooting trees. One more delayed-action bomb fell on Mousehold Heath opposite the War Memorial Cottages and this exploded at 11.22am on 28 October causing slight damage to the cottages. A bungalow on Furze Road, Thorpe, was demolished by a high-explosive bomb and here two people were hurt.

Six more bombs fell in the St Faiths area. These aircraft had come in very low – one eye-witness thought at less than 100 feet. It must have been a harassing experience to see the machine-guns of a low-flying plane pumping bullets on to the residential area of Hellesdon and it seems the more amazing that there was no report of casualties.

At the end of October it was recorded that the siren had sounded 109 times which must have made the running of shops in Norwich exasperating enough without the shoppers' constant grumbles over stock shortages. But the people made do and if they couldn't get it in blue, well, they had it in pink!

Believed to be the first prosecution of its kind under the National Registration Act of 1939, a charge of forging an identity card came before the Norwich Magistrates this week. The defendant, a woman who had been living rough at various camps since the outbreak of war, had recently been found in a destitute condition in an air-raid shelter. She was put on probation for two years and bound over on the understanding that she was neither to associate with soldiers nor frequent camps or billets.

Also during this week the Chief Constable, Mr J H Dain, clarified the position being widely discussed at the time, of people found striking matches in the streets during blackout periods. 'People are not allowed to strike matches in the open at any time during the blackout,' he said; 'it does not matter whether an air-raid warning is in force or not.' These remarks also applied to the use of petrol lighters. There had also been complaints about people striking matches and lighters on the tops of buses during the blackout and this also was stated to be an offence.

Norwich Corporation this month installed at the Harford refuse tip a new £600 tin-baling press and each day it compressed about a ton of tins – salvage from Norwich householders.

The first week of this month the Regent Cinema was showing His Girl Friday, starring Cary Grant and Rosalind Russell. and later in the month at the Haymarket Theatre Laurence Olivier and Joan Fontaine were to be seen in Rebecca. At the Theatre Royal Tom Walls was making a personal appearance in Springtime for Henry.

Raid 9

1 November 1940 (Friday) Alert 19.04 hours

This was a very minor raid, only three incendiary bombs being dropped. Larkman Lane School received one through the lavatory roof and one can but imagine the remarks made by the pupils. The Good Companions public house in Earlham Green Lane received an incendiary in its back garden and this was very quickly smothered with earth by ARP wardens – as Warden's Post G5 was situated at this pub the incendiary must have received very prompt attention.

The third incendiary fell on the roadway outside 242 Earlham Green Lane, and was dealt with by the wardens.

On 10 November Coventry was heavily bombed resulting in the loss of its cathedral. The people of Norwich realized that they could also suffer such a loss.

Raid 10

11 November 1940 (Monday) Alert 04.05 hours

In this raid only incendiary bombs were dropped. The aircraft came in from the north-east and the majority of the bombs fell in roadways and gardens. The only satisfaction to the enemy seems to have been in getting everybody out of bed earlier than usual. The Fire Brigade extinguished

This contingent of Wardens had established their post at the aptly named pub, the Good Companions.

small fires at 45 Vincent Road, 22 and 55 Britannia Road, 6 Matlock Road, and at Care's last works in Victoria Street.

In one of the gardens a mound of earth used to smother one of the incendiary bombs was crowned with a small bunch of violets that had been inadvertently transplanted. An even stranger feature of the raid was a report that two Italian bombers had been shot down in Suffolk and it was thought at the time that these were responsible for the raid on Norwich. This is the only occasion on record of activity over the region by Italian aircraft.

It was during this week that twenty London firemen came to Norwich for two weeks' rest, the same number of Norwich firemen having taken their places in London.

At the Norwich Market chickens were selling at 3s each, ducks from 4s 6d, and chilled salmon from 1s 10d to 2s. After having a meal, to help feed the pigs and poultry owned by farmers in near-by country areas, you were encouraged to place your scraps in one of the Food Scrap Bins. Nothing was wasted. The Ministry of Food in the week's 'Food Facts' recommended that the juice from swedes and turnips be substituted for orange juice as an added source of vitamins for babies.

In November a well-known multiple tailor in Magdalen Street announced that they had continued to sell their made-to-measure suits for 30s for over a year after war was declared, as their contribution to the Government's wish to keep down the cost of living. However, they feared that when their present stocks were exhausted they would have to charge 39s including tax.

Raid 11

2 December 1940 (Monday) Alert 17.40 hours

Fog hung over the City on this Monday evening as a single plane dropped a number of small high-explosive bombs. Possibly because of the blanket of fog, the whistle from these falling bombs was heard over a wide area.

The Cathedral Cloisters rocked as a bomb exploded, cracking buttresses and leaving a crater 15 feet by five feet. In the Cathedral proper, blast broke leaded windows to a height of 60 feet. Another bomb fell in the space between the north transept and the Bishop's Palace. This

Food Facts No 103, one of a series issued by the Ministry of Food

bomb, failing to explode, hit the brick covering of a disused well and disappeared into the sandy soil below. Men of the Royal Engineers sandbagged the area round the well in case the bomb was near the surface, and then started the job of digging it out. As the sand was removed the bomb sank lower and lower and when the diggers reached water the attempt to remove it was abandoned. A further bomb in the garden of 6 The Close made a small crater but did no damage.

In the backyard of 34 Prince of Wales Road electric mains were damaged and an outhouse and garage in the passageway of Vedast Street were demolished. The front garden of 49a Sycamore Villas behind Rose Lane was hit by a bomb that caused a large crater, which in turn engulfed one Anderson shelter and damaged another; there were no casualties. Numbers 43, 45 and 47 St John Street were demolished and air-raid wardens assisted the Rescue Party in helping people free themselves from these cottages where four people lost their lives and two more were seriously injured.

The Orchard Tavern public house in Mountergate Street was badly damaged when a bomb landed in the roadway. The wife of the licensee and her family were having tea when they heard the bomb whistling down. They ran into the bar intending to go down to the cellar but they

Morgans Brewery, King Street. With war-time beer shortages this was the final straw.

didn't quite make it. The bomb exploded and all the front of the bar came in on them, but by an amazing piece of luck a large beam just over their heads remained in position and they were able to scramble out unhurt.

Morgan's Brewery in Synagogue Street had the centre of its building demolished and three soldiers walking past at the time had to watch as beer ran in a river at their feet. One turned to the other and with feeling in his voice said, 'Do you know you've got tears running down your cheeks?' – understandable when beer was in such short supply.

A heap of coal in Coller's coal yard in St Ann's Lane erupted, mushroomed, and then fell back to refill the crater, and the same thing happened in Moy's coal yard in King Street. The warehouses of Corona and Oxo, also in King Street, were partially damaged and numbers 226 and 228 were demolished, the ruins breaking into flames an hour later.

A lorry-driver from Wymondham was travelling along Riverside when a bomb exploded and the road opened up before him. His lorry plunged into the crater but he managed to scramble out unhurt.

In the garden of Hildersham House in Ice House Lane a bomb exploded but caused little damage. In Braconsdale, Arley House was demolished but luckily was unoccupied at the time and water-mains were damaged as a bomb crashed into the roadway opposite number 58. This last bomb also caused some damage to a public air-raid shelter and, sadly, the death of Sergeant Arthur John Pennymore of the Special Constabulary who was

The Orchard Tavern in Mountergate, scene of a remarkable escape during Raid 11.

However familiar such scenes as these became, they still managed to collect a small crowd of onlookers. This picture was taken in King Street.

walking past at the time.

Unexploded bombs often proved difficult to identify for in many cases they caused severe structural damage to property and often gave the impression that an explosion had in fact occurred. Conversely, many lightly damaged houses were suspected of housing unexploded bombs and this in fact happened at 11 Stuart Road where there was thought to be a delayed-action bomb. The area was evacuated but given a clean bill of health by the Military when it was later discovered that the bomb had already exploded.

The London Philharmonic Orchestra paid a surprise visit to Norwich on the Tuesday of this week and gave two concerts in St Andrew's Hall which were conducted by Mr Basil Cameron. There was a very large attendance at both the afternoon and evening performances. At the Theatre Royal Emlyn Williams and Angela Baddeley were appearing in The Light of Heart.

Raid 12

11 December 1940 (Wednesday) No Alert

On a cold December morning, with no siren wailing to alert the citizenry, a lone raider circled the City.

On Carrow Hill at 10 Carrow Vale, in a small terrace of cottages nestling at the bottom of the hill, lived William Warnes, an 83 year old pensioner. As the bomb landed on his house the blast hurled him, complete with bed, into the front garden and there, surrounded by piles of debris, he lay. Apart from shock he was unhurt. Opposite the Warnes lived E S West, a Leading Fireman in the Auxiliary Fire Service, and a man with a knowledge of First Aid. On hearing the noise of the explosion and the whine of missiles passing over his own roof, he rushed to his front door and on opening it was horror-struck by the scene that met his eyes. He knew the Warnes family and that Mr Warnes, a fiery old gentleman, had refused to sleep downstairs along with his daughter and grand-daughter. Mr West rushed across the road and realized that one of the piles of debris was Mr Warnes in his bed. Satisfying himself that the old man was not badly hurt he crawled and wormed his way, by the dimmed light of a pocket-torch, through what was left of the front of the house with the adjoining walls threatening to collapse at any moment. He looked for, and found, Mr Warnes's daughter and grand-daughter. The daughter was injured but alive. The grand-daughter, a girl of 18, was dead. Mr West pulled the daughter to safety as further bombs crashed down. These fell in the grounds of Carrow Abbey and caused no damage.

Mr Warnes, before retirement, had worked at Colmans' Carrow Works where Mr West was presently employed. As so often happened in these raids the helping hands of neighbour and workmate were always there. Mr West was awarded the King's Commendation for Brave Conduct and later he was to receive the Civil Defence Long Service Medal.

Mr West, an employee of Colmans', was a member of their Air Raid Spotters, a private organization supplementing the public warning system, which Colmans' had created jointly with Boulton & Paul's and Laurence, Scott & Electromotors. These firms had pooled resources and built spotting posts, and they had their own internal air-raid signal system. Because of the high number of public warnings in August 1940, totalling some 112 hours, Laurence, Scott decided in September to carry on working throughout public warnings and rely solely on their own spotters. As time went on more and more workers carried on as confidence in their own spotters grew.

On Monday 16 December a most unfortunate incident occurred when one of our own planes dropped bombs in the Dereham Road area. One of these bombs fell on Howes' garage in Bond Street.

Raid 13

21 December 1940 (Saturday) Alert 17.19 hours

The air throbbed with the noise of enemy aircraft as wave after wave of bombers flew over the City. From 5.19pm on the Saturday until 4.45am on the Sunday could be heard, at intervals, the steady passage of planes.

This time the City was not the target but it seems that one of the enemy could not resist the temptation and at 11.15pm a bomb fell at Rye Avenue causing the roadway to erupt, a fractured water-main to gush fountains of water, and fumes from a broken gas-main to drift through the air. There was only one minor casualty and a few houses suffered light damage. A delayed-action bomb fell through the trees into Bracondale Woods and air-raid wardens made an intensive search. They probed at the ground through the cold winter's night but it was not until 4.51am on the Sunday that a shout rang out indicating that it had been located.

During 1940 there had been a total of 580 Alerts lasting in all 640 hours 19 minutes.

The year was drawing to a close and with Christmas only a few days away

Carrow Hill, scene of a famous incident during Raid 12, when Mr William Warnes, the 83 year old resident of this cottage, had his bed blown into the road with himself still in it.

the Government announced there were to be extra rations – 12oz sugar, 4oz tea – and a rumour went round that some shops would be selling oranges. Christmas drink had to be collected: Irish and Scotch whisky was 15s 9d a large bottle, fine pale sherry 6s 4d a bottle, and vintage 1928 champagne 10s 6d a bottle. Christmas mail would arrive on time as the Post Office had taken on 30 extra postwomen. Norwich City Football Team was to play Brighton on Christmas Day, kick-off at 11am. This year's pantomime, Red Riding Hood, was to open on Boxing Day and, as a Christmas treat, you could go in the 3s 6d and not the usual 1s seats.

Your ration book was essential to you if you needed clothes or food.

Raid 14

5 January 1941 (Sunday) Alert 10.38 hours

New Year's Eve had come and gone and it was five days into 1941 when the sirens' painful wail was heard in the City as a single enemy aircraft came in from the south-west. Its bombs fell on the outskirts of the City and its machine-guns pumped bullets along Ampthill Street and Unthank Road causing surprisingly little damage. The pilot released his bombs after diving down to 100 feet and they fell on the City of Norwich School's playing-fields and the Eaton Golf Course. Sixteen in all, they were very evenly spaced, 20 to 100 yards apart, causing craters six feet deep. No doubt the golfers in no way appreciated these additional German-made bunkers. The last bomb fell 30 yards from the east end of the City of Norwich School, the only damage being broken windows.

This week Norwich City Football Club were feeling very hard done by; they had not been given a match fixture for five weeks and felt the London clubs were giving them a raw deal. At the Castle Museum members of HM Forces stationed in East Anglia were holding an exhibition of art. The paper spoke of the high standard of their work and noted 'among the drawings, those of Ronald Searle are of high merit'.

One item of news met with much approval. Beer was not to be rationed. That was officially, but the limitation of supplies from the brewers to the public houses made it inevitable that a form of rationing had to be maintained by the landlords who should have been forgiven for looking after their regulars, but seldom were.

Still, the January sales were on and there were some good bargains in the shops. One store had a good supply of winter coats for £1, and a number of dresses at 10s and some way-out hats for 2s 6d each.

This week the Theatre Royal rang with the laughter of a hundred evacuee children. This particular group living in Costessey came to the pantomime through the generosity of a Costessey couple. Some of these children came from London's Dockland and had never been to a theatre. Seldom has Red Riding Hood been so enjoyed.

Another good thing this week: artisans in the City heard that they could get grants to replace their tools of trade if they were lost in air raids.

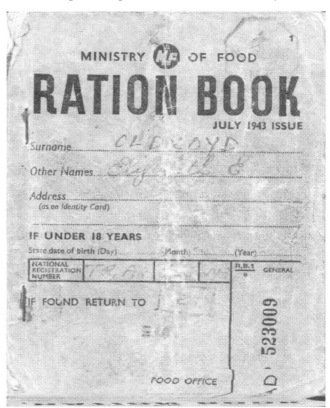

The war had now been on for well over a year and if the blackout curtains were a little thin, not to worry, the shops had a supply of good black twill in at 1s 3d a yard. As it was January the blackout lasted a very long time – from 5.35pm to 8.36am – but if you got a bit depressed with it all then the Samson & Hercules ballroom had their usual dance from 7.30 to 11.30pm Of course, the place would be jammed to the doors – but who cared!

Raid 15

4 February 1941 (Tuesday) Alert 18.29 hours

The Alert sounded as enemy aircraft approached from a northerly direction. High-explosive bombs were dropped on two houses and two bungalows and blast damaged several other properties.

Mrs Brown and her mother of 58 Womersley Road had a remarkable escape. Both ladies were sitting in a downstairs room knitting when the ceiling collapsed. Fortunately the joists and ceiling tilted forward intact thus leaving a cavity where the two ladies were sitting and apart from a cut to Mrs Brown's head they escaped unhurt.

Another bomb fell between 60 and 62 Womersley Road and blast caused damage to doors and windows. In Plumstead Road, number 104 was completely demolished and two bungalows, numbers 91 and 93, were also destroyed. Seven bombs hit Hilary Avenue, six of these landing on the road and in gardens. Those on the road damaged water-mains, but apart from broken windows very little other damage was done. Seven more bombs fell across Edwards's Quarry and Valley Drive; all making craters some six feet in diameter. Boulton & Paul's Dispatch Department also suffered considerable damage.

During this raid seven people were injured, two fatally.

Raid 16

18 February 1941 (Tuesday) Alert 23.19 hours

A number of aircraft passed over the City during the night and in the early hours of the morning at five past five one dropped a large explosive missile on a heavily populated district of small houses and shops. There was a terrific explosion, followed by a dense cloud of smoke. Wardens and rescue workers rushed to the scene and a van arrived filled with members of the police force who, on tumbling out, stopped, frozen by the outrage before their eyes. The area of devastation was greater than anything yet seen in Norwich. The rows of houses around what was left of the Vauxhall

Tavern public house were twisted and torn into piles of rubble and rescue workers, wardens and neighbours tore at the heaps of bricks to release the injured and the dying. Their task seemed impossible.

Both sides of Vauxhall Street from numbers 40 to 60 and from numbers 45 to 51 were wrecked, and blast had extensively damaged some 36

Just one rug and four pictures seem to be the only things left of a home in Vauxhall Street.

cottages in Horace Street, Walpole Street, and Coach & Horses Street. People were standing dazed in front of their homes, which in many cases were too dangerous to enter, and the police helped and advised wherever they could. It was found that 140 people had been rendered homeless and these were sent to Bignold School Rest Centre as a temporary measure until other accommodation could be found.

By daylight mobile canteens were on the spot supplying food and hot drinks to grey, soot-covered figures, and everybody helped his neighbour. Along the street in the early morning came the wonderful smell of newly baked bread. The small bakery of Mr and Mrs Potter in Rupert Street, only a short distance from the crater, had survived. Mr Potter and his son had helped with the rescue, carrying old people from their wrecked houses, and when they returned home they found their bake-office in complete disarray. But the wall ovens were undamaged, so crisp bread was baked and handed out to the tired rescue workers and shaken neighbours. How welcome it must have been!

There was to be much speculation about this bomb in the weeks that followed. One theory was that it had been a mine – the vast area of devastation and the size of the crater pointed to a parachute mine. But there was never a shred of parachute found and this was strange, as something usually survived. The parachute mine was a gruesome weapon of its day.

Tea assumed a new importance in wartime and could be a lifesaver on occasions. This photograph was taken in Walpole Street after Raid 16.

Cylindrical in shape it measured 2 feet 2 inches in diameter and from 5 feet 8 inches to 8 feet 8 inches in length. Its parachute would be from 23 to 27 feet in diameter and 24 to 28 cords held it to the missile. The weight of the charge ranged from 776 to 1,536 lb.

Another theory was that this had been a very large bomb that had exploded on impact. The Germans were known to have the 1,800 kg 'Satan' bomb and the even larger 2,500 kg 'Max' bomb, but British Intelligence had no details of the latter or of the 3,500 kg bomb that was known to be in production. There was also a 'G'-type mine: 6 feet 4 inches long, painted sky-blue, with a tailfin made of Bakelised paper. This mine fell without a parachute, had a 1,618 lb charge, and a total weight of 2,160 lbs. One wonders which of these weapons caused the devastation in Vauxhall Street – the only certain thing was that this had been no ordinary bomb.

Raid 17

27 February 1941 (Thursday) Alert 10.09 hours

Visibility on this grey morning was bad with clouds forming a ceiling at less than 400 feet over Barnards' factory at Mousehold. From overhead a Heinkel 111 dived, levelling out at 200 feet. The shrill note of the warning siren, the crash of the first bombs, the thunder of guns from nearby Mousehold Aerodrome, and the crackle of the Heinkel's machine-guns, sounded almost simultaneously.

Alfred Malcolm Parslow, an 18 year old plane-spotter situated high above the ground in a crow's nest, saw the plane flying directly towards him, its machine-guns pumping out bullets. His only protection was a canvas screen but, knowing he was in grave danger, he kept his head, stood firm, and carried on with his duties. For this act he was later commended for gallantry.

Back on the ground some of the employees rushed to their shelters but the majority flung themselves under anything that offered protection. All the time the incessant crackling of the bomber's machine-guns could be heard. As in an earlier raid on Barnards, the bombs fell on to the centre of buildings which, happily, were empty of both employees and plant. There were many near-escapes from the machine-gunning; the wonder being that nobody was killed. Edmund (Nobby) Clarke, an employee of the company for sixty years, and Wilfred Burton, a netting-weaver, began to run for the shelter. Burton turned back to seek cover in a doorway but Nobby, seeing sparks spurting from the ground, threw himself down and pulled his overcoat over his head. His only injury was a small cut on the scalp probably from a splinter of glass or wood. William Le Neve Bower, Junior Works Manager, rushed out of the office block to be met with a downpour of bullets and splinters. He darted back not expecting to reach cover alive but the searching bullets failed to find him.

The effect of blast and concussion was unpredictable and frequently damage occurred which was inexplicable. For example roof lights within 40 feet of the centre of the explosion remained unbroken yet at the far side of the building windows were shattered and stretches of guttering were thrown to the ground. In a lean-to office the blast sucked in parts of the roof, dislodging three heavy weights which in falling narrowly missed the prone bodies of two sheltering employees. Members of the Works ARP Unit and other employees were quickly on the scene but their services were hardly called for. Production at the factory was not interfered with and everyone was relieved to learn there had been no serious injury to personnel.

This week it was learnt that a small quantity of oranges had arrived in the City but they were not to be seen on display in the shops and many a hopeful housewife searched in vain. The shop-keepers had hurriedly put these luxuries under the counter for their Registered customers, as they did with so many things in short supply. One surprising thing was noticeable: considering the opportunities offered by the blackout there had been no general increase in crime. This must have been gratifying; you could at least hold on to the things you had got.

Raid 18

14/15 March 1941 (Friday) Alert 20.08 hours

In this raid a solitary aircraft scattered some 50 incendiary bombs over a wide area. Luckily most of them fell on roads and gardens and caused only small fires. The most serious fire occurred at Raob Yard in Colegate Street when an incendiary bomb penetrated a garage roof and fell on to

a car. The car was a write-off but the Fire Brigade managed to save the garage. A 14th century house in The Close, number 57, had a bomb fall in the central valley of the roof causing slight damage and melting a square of lead before being extinguished. A gentlemen's outfitters at 3 Magdalen Street had another incendiary which the ARP wardens quickly got under control. At 54 Magdalen Close an incendiary was reported by the City's Chief Warden, Mr V E Harrison, and this was quickly dealt with by one of his force. At Southall's shoe factory in Crome Road an incendiary bomb was quickly extinguished, but a lot of damage was done because the fire-watchers were unable to turn off the sprinkler system.

To illustrate the scattered nature of the attack an incendiary bomb fell on 5 Brown's Buildings in West Pottergate Street where it penetrated the roof and fell onto a bed. At the same time several bombs fell on allotments at the rear of Gertrude Road.

The National Wheat Loaf was launched this month and it was loudly acclaimed by the Government as the most nourishing bread there could be, not as dark as brown and not as white as white, but very good for you. They didn't say in the paper if it would make you put weight on and this was important because if you only had a few clothing coupons left then last year's dress would have to be trimmed, dyed, or in some way altered to look different because you wanted to go to the Lido dance-hall that night.

On the outbreak of war Bert Galey and his Band were resident at the Lido. Mr Galey, a well-known local band-leader, played for dances until 1940 when he became the Manager of the dance-hall and Eddie Gates and his Band took over. Mr Gates, a totally blind man, gave much pleasure to many dancers and often continued playing through many of the worst air raids. After Eddie Gates, Dorothy Bridges, or 'Dolly' as she was known, took over with her band. She was a competent musician having obtained a very comprehensive training playing at the Haymarket Theatre in the days of silent films. At a later stage of the war Billie Duncan and his Band were to play their pounding rhythm to delight the jitterbugging revellers.

Mr V E Harrison who was also the City's Chief Warden owned the Lido throughout these years. He controlled the Wardens throughout the war years and was later to receive the MBE for his services to Civil Defence. Mr Harrison was also the owner or controller of a number of cinemas in the County and of the Regal, Capitol, and Ritz in the City and his services to entertainment were very much appreciated in wartime when any diversion to lighten the gloom of austerity was so essential.

Outside the Lido the queues were long but Mrs (Nellie) Scott, the tiny dark-haired lady cashier whose hands flew so quickly over the piles of change, was there to greet you, asking after your welfare, often using your Christian name. She also frequently made up the price of a ticket if a British Serviceman didn't have quite enough to buy his way in. Mrs Gallant and her daughter Jean will also be remembered at the cash-desk as will Jock, the big uniformed doorman, who hurried you through into the dance-hall proper. The men will remember George the one-armed cloakroom attendant. Once inside, the large ball of mirrors hanging from the roof slowly rotated reflecting the tiny beams of light and illuminating the dance-floor where the girls danced in the arms of British, Czech, Polish, American, Australian, Dutch, Canadian, or French Servicemen. The siren may have sounded but the war seemed miles away. When tired or hot from the crush you walked to the balcony to sit and watch the dancers and wondered how your friend could always make her clothing coupons go so much further than yours. At the buffet Mrs Richards, Mrs Galey, Mrs Barrett, or Mrs Norman would be serving, trying to make some sort of display out of their limited supplies. The Lido dance-hall of Norwich was to be remembered by many people all over the world for many years after the war and the bands and staff were to be very much a part of that memory.

Raid 19

30/31 March 1941 (Sunday/Monday)
First Alert 21.11 hours, second Alert 00.53 hours

It was about 10.30pm when a plane dropped bombs near railway lines close by Mile Cross Bridge and in the grounds of the Waterworks. They fell in soft ground, exploded, and made large craters but did no damage. The All Clear sounded at 27 minutes past midnight only for the alert to be sounded again 26 minutes later, by which time the people of Norwich must have been fed up. In this second attack bombs fell on Caernarvon Road and Earlham Road.

At 130 Earlham Road the occupier escaped uninjured as the back of his house was demolished, but his two young sons were trapped. Debris poured into their bedroom, most of it falling on to the younger boy's bed. Only 14 years old, he was protected by a wardrobe which fell across the bed forming a roof over him. Rescue parties and wardens helped release

Bomb damage at the goods yard of Norwich Thorpe station.

both the boys, and when a small fire broke out it was quickly extinguished. Mr Bush, Deputy Warden of Post H3 which was situated at the end of St Thomas Road, was commended for his work in this rescue.

Caernarvon Road was hit by a bomb which left a crater ten feet across and damaged water-mains, gas-mains, and overhead telephone lines.

Raid 20

2 April 1941 (Wednesday) Alert 14.22 hours

One minute after a second Alert had sounded, a Dornier 215 approached in a shallow dive, dropping from 1,500 feet to approximately 900 feet. Cloud was low and visibility poor. Two large high-explosive bombs were dropped. One fell at Thorpe Station hitting numbers One and Two Goods Yards damaging several trucks and causing one fatality. The other fell on wasteland close by, causing no damage. The film showing at the Odeon, starring Richard Dix and Wendy Barrie, was entitled Men Against the Sky which must have had an ironic ring.

Norwich schoolchildren and their teachers were this week wearing their gas-masks for short periods during lessons to help familiarize themselves with their use.

At Morse's Cringleford nurseries women land-workers who for years had helped in the cultivation of roses, were now busy growing vegetables. Some 400 acres previously used for rose culture had now been put down to vegetables to help fill the national larder.

This week the 1941 Budget introduced a new form of income tax – 'Pay As You Earn'. This would bring the war much nearer to the many families who had hitherto escaped any direct financial levy. The Chancellor of the Exchequer's new tax, though severe, had been accepted with surprisingly little criticism – men and women seemed prepared to sacrifice a good deal in order to beat 'Hitlerism'.

At the Theatre Royal you could see what was described as 'the brightest touring show' called All Clear with Elsie Prince and Buck and Chic as part of an all-star company. At the Haymarket Theatre you could see Arthur Askey and Richard Murdoch in The Ghost Train.

Raid 21

29 April 1941 (Tuesday) Alert 21.55 hours

A warm spring evening and at ten o' clock, five minutes after the Alert had sounded, the factory sirens gave their warning. Seven minutes later major fires and a great deal of damage was caused as high-explosive and incendiary bombs were dropped. Considering the amount of damage done the casualty list was surprisingly low there seems to have been only one fatality. Some of the incendiaries fell on Laurence, Scott & Electromotors, Boulton & Paul's, and houses in the adjoining roads all were immediately extinguished.

Four bombs fell on Colmans' Carrow Works in King Street, and were thought to be oil bombs. These oil bombs were 5 feet 5 inches long, 2 feet across the fin area, and 1 foot 11 inches at the nose. They had a nitroglycerine burster charge and contained 30 gallons of oil. These fell on the Waverley Oats and Flour Mills. There was an immediate outbreak of fire in both mills which quickly developed into a major incident. The Carrow Works Fire Brigade, augmented by the City Fire Brigade and the Auxiliary Fire Service were engaged in fighting the blaze for five hours before the outbreak was brought under control and although the brigades worked unceasingly both mills were gutted.

At the corner of Winkles Row in King Street, a high-explosive bomb demolished 1 Winkles Road and 272 King Street. Another fell on some

Messrs Colman's, King Street. A shell is all that is left.

outbuildings demolishing by blast 3 and 4 Cinder Ovens Row and here a minor fire was extinguished with stirrup pumps. One bomb fell in the Wilderness in King Street, causing no damage. Two more high-explosive bombs fell in the roadway at Carrow Hill and these caused craters which set fire to gas-mains and damaged water-mains.

The whole sky was red with the reflection of these fires and the streets clouded by smoke, as Mr Harry Lyons volunteered to drive to the Fire Station to pilot trailer-pumps to the scene of the biggest fires. As he drove along his car suddenly plunged into one of the craters. He sustained cuts to his nose and forehead but he immediately secured another car and insisted on completing his mission before going to hospital.

28 Bracondale had extensive damage from a bomb that fell at the rear of the house and two more bombs were to fall on Bracondale that night: one in the roadway, damaging water-mains, and the other at the rear of number 13 where a number of houses were severely damaged by blast.

Yet another gas-main was damaged as bombs hit City Road where number 17 was demolished by blast which also caused extensive damage to adjoining properties. A high-explosive bomb landed at the rear of Kensington Row, demolishing number 13 and damaging other houses. Youell Opening in Hall Road had one cottage destroyed with the adjoining one partially demolished. A bomb that fell on Alan Road luckily failed to explode. The immediate area was evacuated and the bomb later removed by the Bomb Disposal Unit. Another delayed-action bomb fell in the roadway near Surrey Street Bus Station and this was removed the next day.

A high-explosive bomb, with an incendiary attached to it, fell on 26 St Faith's Lane, penetrating to the ground floor. The bomb failed to explode but the incendiary ignited. The high-explosive bomb was not discovered until after the incendiary had been dealt with. One more delayed-action bomb was to fall on the Bowling Green at the rear of the Norfolk & Norwich Comrades Club in St Faith's Lane and this was not discovered until the following morning. When it was dug up this was also found to have an incendiary wired to the fins.

Raid 22

6 May 1941 (Tuesday) Alert 22.42 hours

Hostile aircraft dropped a number of high-explosive and incendiary bombs. Although the high-explosive bombs were of a small calibre they had a very powerful blast effect and extensive damage was caused. Doors and windows were damaged in over a hundred houses and 20 of them were made untenable.

Wardens' Post.

In the garden of 155 Unthank Road a high-explosive bomb caused severe damage. The fronts of numbers 153 and 155 collapsed and many shops and houses in the vicinity were damaged by blast.

Warden Townsend from Post O2 (situated in St Gregory's Alley) reported a number of small incidents at St Gregory's Church, Bullard's Anchor Brewery in Coslany Street, and Stamp Office Yard in St Andrew Street. Warden Holt of post F4 (situated in Newmarket Street) and a Sergeant of the Special Constabulary reported incidents in Bury Street. These were later found to have been caused by a direct hit on 24 Bury Street, which demolished the house, and by an incendiary bomb that fell among the debris. A further bomb landed in the road opposite 34 Bury Street and although it made only a small crater extensive damage was done to adjacent property.

Further reports of occurrences that night were to come from Post G6 (situated in The Avenues) where Warden Evans reported incendiaries in Christchurch Road, Jessopp Road, Avenue Road, and Heigham Park. Warden Oswick of Post G1 (situated at Clarendon Steps off Clarendon Road) reported an incident at 1 Chester Place and Warden Townsend of O2 Post also reported one at St George Street outside St Andrew's Hall.

The Wardens' Service consisted of many posts dotted around the City giving a complete coverage for spotting and reporting bomb attacks (see Appendix 2).

Raid 23

7 May 1941 (Wednesday) Alert 21.56 hours

A white light was seen to be showing from the enemy plane which at 35 minutes to midnight dropped 24 bombs in the Larkman Lane School area. One fell on the school itself, two made direct hits on Council houses and the rest fell in gardens and roads. Blast caused extensive damage and 150 people were rendered homeless. These unfortunates were accommodated for the night at Colman Road Rest Centre.

Number 47 Cadge Road, the home of the Britcher family, felt the full tragedy of this raid. Mr and Mrs Britcher and three of their children were killed outright and their remaining three children suffered serious injuries as the house collapsed on them. They were later dug out by a rescue squad. This was an extraordinary escape; no one expected to find anybody alive. The blast from this bomb also damaged the roofs and bedrooms of neighbouring houses. Five bombs in all fell in the gardens of this road causing considerable damage.

The Britchers' neighbours, the Robinsons, had a remarkable escape. The family of seven suffered only superficial injuries although two of the boys were buried beneath the bricks and mortar of their home. The ceil-

ing of the bedroom fell on Mr and Mrs Robinson and on their youngest son's bed.

Six more bombs fell near shops, houses, and a Sunday school at the junction of Cadge Road and Earlham Grove and considerable damage was done. There were some casualties and many cases of cuts and bruises.

A direct hit on 5 Bixley Close partially demolished the house and two more bombs fell in the gardens. Blast from another bomb in a wood 150 yards to the west side of The Good Companions public house in Earlham Green Lane damaged 20 houses and brought down overhead electric cables, injuring seven people.

In this raid the bombs appeared to have been dropped in a circular pattern within a radius of half a mile.

The rich voice of Richard Tauber, the world-famous tenor, could be heard at the Theatre Royal. The drab greyness the war had brought to the City, the peeling paintwork, the worn colourless clothes, were forgotten for a while by the audiences who packed the theatre.

At the Rotary Club this week a much more down to earth subject was being discussed – rats! Some startling statistics relating to the activities of rats were given. Loss and damage caused by these vermin was at any time incalculable but in wartime it became a matter of great importance as these rodents were ranged on the side of the enemy. The speaker alluded to rats and mice as the 'sixth column under the floor' and said that the food intake of a rat was about 1 oz per day.

A call was made for more voluntary fire-watchers and judging by the general response the citizens had realized the importance of this section of the ARP.

Raid 24

10 May 1941 (Saturday) Alert 00.08 hours

The sound of an enemy aircraft was heard circling the City and at 27 minutes past two, four high-explosive bombs fell.

One bomb made a direct hit on the top-floor flat at 4 Lady Betty Road but as the occupiers were away there were no casualties. Blast from this bomb blew in the door of the electricity substation in Lady Betty Road

Brick surface Wardens' Post, Woodcock Close. A near miss: with a poster of Winston Churchill on the wall, maybe the bomb thought better of it?

without damage to the installation while several other houses in the vicinity were also damaged by blast. In the centre of Cecil Road, just westward of Grove Walk, a bomb made a crater, damaged a number of houses, and blew off the door of Wardens' Post E5.

At 19 Ipswich Road another bomb destroyed a lean-to shed. Finally, a bomb fell at the rear of Heathfield House in Ipswich Road and 20 Lime Tree Road causing blast damage to roofs and windows.

Sadly, on 12 May this week, the first case of looting was heard at the Magistrates' Court, the culprit being found guilty and fined £5.

At the Carlton Cinema George Formby was starring in It's in the Air.

The Home Guard were busy learning a new method of fighting. They were being trained in an unscrupulous form of ju-jitsu, 'a cross between unarmed combat and antagonistics, body balance being the underlying principle'.

At the Haymarket Theatre the National Baby Welfare Council were showing The Birth of a Baby – no person under the age of 16 being admitted unless accompanied by an adult.

Shattered pieces of bomb like these (seen with a modern 2p piece to indicate their size) would be red hot and fly in all directions, causing great injury and destruction.

Raid 25

17 May 1941 (Saturday) Alert 22.52 hours

Yet again in this month of May the bombers came – this time approaching the City from a north-easterly direction. Two large 2,500 kg bombs fell on marshland near Lakenham Swimming Baths, about 10 yards inside the City boundary. The blast was terrific and caused extensive damage to the windows and roofs of approximately 400 houses on the Lakenham Council Estate. The inhabitants, and the authorities too, must have been thankful that these large bombs had not hit the estate directly as the loss of life would have been great and the damage would have been extensive.

A warning to the public of the danger which might arise as a result of interfering with unknown objects found on the ground, whether out of curiosity or during souvenir-hunting (which was forbidden), was issued by the Eastern Ministry of Information. The Ministry stated that not only was a person liable to injure himself but in tampering with an unknown object he may very well be doing a disservice to his country by preventing the collection of valuable technical information.

At the Police Court on the Wednesday of this week a defendant whose car containing a shotgun had been found unattended on Orford Hill explained that he carried the gun in case he met enemy parachutists. The Magistrate seemed unimpressed with this plea and fined him.

If the hopes of a number of people in Norwich, Ontario, had been fulfilled many citizens of Norwich, Norfolk, would this year have consumed vegetables grown from seeds sent from Canada. However, enemy action thwarted this kindly idea. The seeds, boxed and addressed to the Lord Mayor of Norwich (Mr B J Hanly) for distribution among would-be gardeners, left Canada but never arrived – they were lost in the Atlantic.

Raid 26

30 July 1941 (Wednesday)
Alert 00.15 hours

Only one bomb fell in this raid and this landed in Wyre Woods in Marl Pit Lane, the only casualty being an uprooted tree.

This evening the Norwich Police Concert Party gave the hundredth performance of their show Front Line Follies 1941. Since the outbreak of war they had given 99 shows and had entertained 8,000 civilians, members of the Civil Defence Services, munitions workers, etc. Tonight the proceeds were to be given to the dependants of casualties on HMS Hood. Not all the police force could have been involved in the concert, for the first prosecutions for failing to produce an Identity Card within the regulation two days were being heard, one person being fined 5s.

There was plenty of other entertainment in

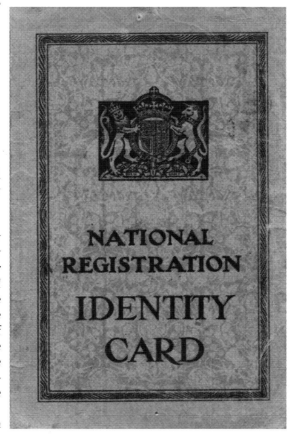

the City tonight. Boxing enthusiasts were attending a fight between Ginger Sadd the well-known Norwich middleweight and Jack Sharkey (no relation of the former American champion). This was to be in aid of 'Tank Week'.

A more sombre activity was taking place at a number of City schools where Mobile Gas Vans were parked and where qualified ARP instructors gave members of the public elementary anti-gas training. Members of the public could pass through the gas-filled room if over the age of eight. These vans were to be parked at 18 different schools during the months of July and August.

Raid 27

8 August 1941 (Thursday)
Alert 22.43

Although the Alert sounded at 10.43pm it was not until five minutes past midnight that a plane began slowly to circle the City. It did three circuits before an RAF night fighter appeared on the scene. Machine-gun fire was heard and the enemy aircraft immediately jettisoned its bomb-load and made off. These bombs, eight in all, fell within a small radius at Church Farm, Eaton, and failed to explode. As they fell in an enclosed area they were not discovered until daybreak by a farm employee. This was the last raid of 1941 and the City was to have a respite of many months. The year 1941 had been a record year for the number of Alerts sounded, in all 673 with a total duration of 1,071 hours. March had had the highest monthly figure of 145 Alerts totalling 177 hours. The longest single Alert was from 6.48pm on Monday 10 February until 6.59am the following day, a period of 12 hours 11 minutes.

All citizens had to carry a card. (The inside looked like the one illustrated on page 42.)

A chance to see the enemy at close quarters as a Dornier 17 was placed on exhibition at Eaton Park.

Norfolk and Norwich Licensed Victuallers' Association this week reached agreement on the question of minimum opening hours for public houses. The majority of the brewers were asking landlords to open every day and ration their supplies of beer – the suggested hours of opening were from noon to 2pm and from 8 to 10pm – they felt that this would prevent people rushing from one licensed house to another.

The Home Guard was growing in strength and could now have a full-time Adjutant and Quartermaster for each battalion of 1,000 men.

The Norwich Air Raid Spotters' Club was formed this month. The object of the Club was to increase the efficiency of spotters in detecting and identifying aircraft. They met at 7.30pm on the second Monday of each month at the ARP Club in Davey Place.

In September a captured Dornier 17 was placed on exhibition at Eaton Park. Also in September it was announced that no drinks were to be served at the City's dance-halls during air raids.

In October £323, 000 was collected during War Weapons Week and the target figure was raised to £1,000,000.

In the evenings people would sometimes listen to William Joyce, or 'Lord Haw-Haw' as he was nicknamed, giving his propaganda programme from Germany. Far from striking fear in the hearts of his listeners these pro-

grammes were a constant source of amusement and when his nasal voice was heard saying 'Jairmany calling, Jairmany calling', in pub and parlour people would gather round their wireless sets to have a laugh. In Norwich on one occasion, however, the laughter was a little hollow when he said: 'The people of Norwich have a new City Hall. It isn't paid for yet but never mind, the Luftwaffe will soon put paid to it.' Joyce was captured by British Forces in 1945 and later hanged for high treason.

An Incident

16 September 1941 (Tuesday) 01.19 hours

Report taken from Incident Book, no other details being available.

Position of Occurrence	Reporting Agent	Post
Gladstone Street	Gooderham 1594	H2
Denbigh Road	–	G4
53/55 Waddington Street	Smith 1607	H7
Nile Street and Nelson Street	Rudd 299	H7
Stafford Street	Robbins 674	H2
Adelaide Street	Neil 501	H7
Cambridge Street	Martins 1063	F3
Bathurst Road, Unthank Road	Clifford 1303	G1
Mill Hill Road, Neville Street	Kayne 1189	H1
West Pottergate Street	Cullington	H1
3, Leopold Road	Francis 451	F4

Alexandra Road	Gooderham 1594	H2
Essex Street	–	F2
52 Somerleyton Street	Savage 157	F1
Neville Street	PC John F Flecter (67)	
Park Lane	Hunt 775	G2
41-43 Suffolk Street	Erasmus 319	F2
Opposite Globe Street	Skoyle 477	F2
Salford Street	Skoyle 477	F2
4 Essex Street	Special Constable 252	
Avenue Road	Tanky 1264	G4
28 York Street	Police report	
Rose Valley	Andrews 285	F2
Eaton Road	Special Constable Walker 240	
8 Waddington Street	Graves 1160	H7
Anderson's Yard Corner, Unthank Road and Park Lane	Farroll 22	G2
37, 39, 41 Unthank Road	Miller 11	G1
58 Mount Pleasant	Bannock 946	F4
20 Branksome Close	Police Constable 65	
12 Cardiff Road	Police report	G4
16 Heigham Grove	Police report	
16 West Parade	Division 1, H.Q.II	
Brunswick Road Nursing Home	Norfolk and Norwich Hospital report	
City of Norwich School Grounds	Police report	
66 Alexandra Road	Vine	H2
4,28,56 Mill Hill Road	Police report	
4 Chester Place	Police report	
The Cottage and Tuktaway, Chester Place	Police report	
12 Heigham Grove	Police report	
Heigham Grove Maternity Home	Police report	
Passage between Grosvenor Road and Neville Street	Police report	
31 Grosvenor Road	Police report	
Rear of 41 Unthank Road	Police report	
Children's Block, Norfolk and Norwich Hospital	Norfolk and Norwich Hospital report	
118 Gladstone Street	Vine	H2

Position of Occurrence	Reporting Agent	Post
30 York Street	Freeman 1878	F3
Allen's Lane, Newmarket Road	Nortoss 207	F5
66 St Philips Road	Police report	
31 Onley Street	Police report	
22 Branksome Close	Police report	
168 Nelson Street	Police report	
49 Adelaide Street	Sellors, Div. 1, HQ II	
39/45 West End Street	Police report	
Park Lane Methodist Chapel	Police report	
Eaton Golf Course	Police report	
160 Dereham Road	Police report	
132 Newmarket Road	Police report	
4 Essex Street	Police report	
43 Melrose Road	Police report	
River-bank by Harford Bridge	Police report	
Marshes, south-west river-bank by Harford Bridge	Police report	

Illustrations from an air raid manual on how to tackle a fire caused by an incendiary bomb.

This is a rather remarkable incident report because there are no records of any raids over this period in any of the City's files. A possible explanation is that on this night in September there fell over Norwich a number

INCENDIARY BOMB AND ITS EFFECT

COOLING DOWN AN INCENDIARY BOMB

REMOVING AN INCENDIARY BOMB WITH SCOOP AND RAKE

CONTROLLING AN INCENDIARY BOMB WITH SAND

PLACING INCENDIARY BOMB IN CONTAINER

STIRRUP HAND-PUMP

TWO-HAND PORTABLE MANUAL FIRE-PUMP IN ACTION

ANTI-GAS CLOTHING

A CHAIN OF CANVAS FIRE BUCKETS

Colour reproductions by courtesy of the Imperial Tobacco Co. (of Great Britain and Ireland), Ltd.

of canister-like objects which were linked together by long wires. They draped themselves over trees, shrubs, chimney-pots and lamp-posts.

At first they were thought to be anti-personnel bombs and a number of people did have remarkable escapes as they pulled at the trailing wires which, in some cases, detonated an explosive charge in the canisters. The Bomb Disposal Squad soon removed these objects.

As there had been no enemy air activity these objects must have been dropped accidentally by our own aircraft. It was said at the time that this was one of the boffins' many inventions and the idea was that these canisters, linked by wires, were to be shot from our planes into the path of on-coming enemy aircraft and in theory the wires would entangle themselves round propellers thus exploding the canisters.

There was now to be a period of raid-free nights for nearly eight months.

CITY OF NORWICH.
AIR RAID PRECAUTIONS.
This is to certify that.....................
...RUTH E. HARDY.....
has been appointed one of the Local Authority's Air Raid Wardens and is authorised to carry out the duties of that office on behalf of the Local Authority.
....
Chief Constable.
A.R.27A. SHAW & SONS LTD., FETTER LANE, E.C.4. G 1633

Between July 1940 and August 1941 Norwich had suffered 27 raids. During this period 81 of her citizens were killed, 102 were admitted to hospital, and 192 were slightly injured.

In November 1941 a campaign was launched in Norwich for a band of women to organize a scheme of mutual aid to assist air-raid victims. Intended to co-operate with the ARP and other voluntary organizations, it was to be called the 'Mutual Aid Good Neighbours' Association'. And so 'MAGNA' was born, and Mrs Ruth Hardy accepted the position of Organizer for the City. The operation was planned on the same lines as the Wardens' organization to cover 1,500 streets and roads and 715 yards and courts. An appeal was made for 2,000 street organizers, 80 post organizers, 12 group leaders, and 3 divisional heads. It was hoped to have one organizer in each street to act as a 'Street Mother' and list each of the aged and infirm living there. The 80 post organizers would be attached to Wardens' Posts, with the group leaders and divisional heads administering the scheme.

The sole aim of this organization was to save the lives of bomb-shocked people and to alleviate the distress of the homeless. Mrs Hardy said that many deaths resulting from shock had occurred in blitzed areas and the only way to combat the effects of shock was to apply immediate warmth. 'We want every housewife in Norwich to offer her home temporarily for such a cause,' she said. Invaluable help could be given by good neighbours in their own homes if transport to rest centres and hospitals was rendered difficult.

MAGNA provided warmth, shelter, sympathy, and kindness. Mrs Hardy worked ceaselessly, meetings and training sessions were held in houses, par-ish halls, cinemas, chapels, schools – in fact anywhere that space was available. Members ran whist drives, concerts, and dances to raise funds, and MAGNA grew and grew until 30,000 Norwich women filled its ranks. Each placed in her window the small yellow poster that announced the fact that 'a good neighbour lives here'. Mrs Hardy, if tired, must have been proud.

CITY OF NORWICH CIVIL DEFENCE WARDENS' SERVICE
M.A.G.N.A. EASTER PARTY
Tea, Dance and Social Evening
LADS' CLUB, KING ST.
THURSDAY, 13th APRIL
TICKETS 2/6   6—10 p.m.   Tea 6.15 p.m. Sharp

M.A.G.N.A.

An RAF Blenheim bomber crashed onto the back of houses in Brabazon Avenue. Two teenagers, Reginald Huggett and Jeffrey Bull, pulled the air-gunner from the burning aircraft.

◄ *Mementoes of MAGNA, including a shoulder flash from a uniform.*

◄◄ *Everyone with an official duty needed their Identity Card and a card indicating their authority.*

Raid 28/29

27/28 and 29/30 April 1942 (Monday and Wednesday nights) First Alert 23.21 hours, Second Alert 21.13 hours.

It was on these nights in April that Norwich received its heaviest raids of the war.

These were named 'Baedeker raids' because Norwich appeared in Baedeker's British Isles as a place of historic interest, and it was deliberately bombed for this reason. Norwich people called them 'the blitz' – 'blitz' is the word used to describe heavy raids and the dictionary defines this word as 'intensive attack' or 'to damage or destroy', but only those who lived through a blitz know the true meaning of the word. The true definition of 'blitz' is 'fire, fear, and fatigue'.

On Monday, the night of the first big raid, a bright moon shone over the City. The first two planes, the pathfinders, flew almost leisurely over the City releasing parachute flares as they did so. The flares supplemented the moonlight and the streets appeared as bright as day. The aircraft then went into a shallow dive, dropping incendiary bombs, and firing their machine-guns. Some minutes later a further six aircraft flew in and the deep rhythmic drone of further planes was heard following in their wake as two more formations, each of ten aircraft, approached the City. The first shower of high-explosive bombs fell in very congested areas where small rows of terraced houses were savagely torn apart. Roaring gas-mains, ignited by the explosions, silhouetted the figures of firemen as they feverishly fought to gain control.

Then there was the noise: the scream of falling bombs, the strange rending moans that timber beams make as they tear themselves apart, the cries of frightened children, and the sound of ambulance bells.

Even at this point the word 'blitz' was still undefined but with the coming of dawn, with the streets impassable, with crackling loud-speakers calling on people to boil all drinking-water and with the many families standing by piles of rubble that had once been their homes – perhaps retrieving from the debris a cup or a chair that had miraculously remained intact and which now represented the sum total of their possessions – then one understood the meaning of the word 'BLITZ'!

A scene of devastation in Orford Place on the morning after the main raid.

The cold facts of the great assault on Norwich were as follows: On the Monday night the raid lasted two hours when 185 high-explosive bombs weighing over 50 tons were dropped, killing 162 people and injuring 600 – a light casualty-list considering the tonnage of bombs dropped – and some 84 people were dug out of the mountains of rubble alive.

After one night's respite on the Tuesday the weary citizens had to endure another night of terror on the Wednesday. Once again flares were dropped and the raid that followed developed on similar lines to that of the Monday. This raid lasted almost an hour and a quarter during which time 112 high-explosive bombs were dropped weighing 45 tons, killing 69 people and injuring 89. In this raid a much higher proportion of incendiaries was used and many of these bombs fell on areas of the City already devastated during Monday's raid.

These then are the bare facts. But what of the people on these nights? A Norwich woman remembers those raids. She, her elderly mother, and her small son were crouched under the dining-room table. Her husband, like so many men, was away working in an aircraft factory. As the explosions shook the house and the walls trembled they clung to each other until, after what seemed like hours, the onslaught stopped. The woman crawled from the makeshift shelter, her hands feeling for the door-handle. She opened the door slowly feeling sure that the house must have been hit and that beyond the door would be a void, but to her relief she found her home to be more or less intact. On the Wednesday night the thought of staying under a City roof was too much for them, and mother, child, and grandmother, warmly dressed, started to walk down Ipswich Road, to join the pitiful groups of women and young children, the old and infirm, pushing barrows, prams, and hand-carts, making their way out to the country. Here and there fathers were to be seen with their families, unable to refuse their pleas, and their presence was to deplete the fire-watching service for that night. A loud-speaker van toured the streets appealing for all able-bodied men to remain at their posts and this must have pulled at them, but their act in staying with their families was understandable and very human. The mother, grandmother and boy found that the Eastern Counties Omnibus Company had parked some of their vehicles under the trees in Ipswich Road for safety so with many others they crawled into them and made themselves as comfortable as possible for the rest of the night, returning to their homes next morning to sweep up the broken glass, pull down torn curtains, and attempt to brush away the seemingly endless layers of soot.

On that Monday night a 15 year old girl had been working with her mother at the Lido dance-hall in Aylsham Road, and after a very busy evening was tired and not looking forward to the long walk home to Unthank Road. As the couple left the dance-hall and walked down Aylsham Road the moon was so bright that they had no need to use their torches. As

they approached Junction Road the Alert sounded and they hurried down the hill. From this vantage-point they saw two aircraft diving so low over the Dolphin Bridge that they seemed to be on a level with them. By the light of parachute flares the girl saw bombs tumbling from the two planes. She shouted to her mother 'down' and they lay crouched against a garden wall as the bombs struck. In the lull that followed the urge to get home was their main thought and they ran half crouched towards the Dolphin Bridge. Running over this long narrow footbridge the scream of bombs seemed all round them and the sky was thick with smoke. As they reached Heigham Street, the Dolphin public house was ablaze with flames roaring from every window. Searching in the smoke for an air-raid shelter they stumbled across Heigham Street into Old Palace Road, and in so doing saved their lives, although at the time they had no way of knowing this.

In Old Palace Road they took refuge in a brick surface shelter. The section they had dashed into appeared strangely empty, nevertheless they crouched on the wooden seats with their hands clasped over their ears to shut out the endless explosions. The shelter rocked, and one explosion was so loud they felt it must collapse – they seemed to sit there for hours. After a time sweat formed on their faces and the girl realized this was not caused by fear, the shelter was becoming stiflingly hot. Tentative hands placed on the walls told her that they were heating up and then another

Harmer's clothing factory in St Andrew Street – engaged in making Army uniforms – was hit several times.

Assistant Chief Warden Percy Scott used an exercise book to keep detailed notes at lectures on the different types of bomb. ▶

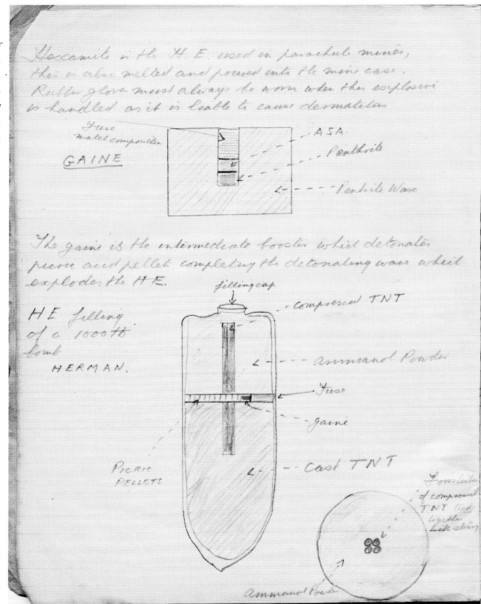

It was important to carry your Identity Card at

explosion made her hands go back to clasping her ears.

Time passed and suddenly the scream of bombs stopped, to be replaced by the sound of crackling flames. As they left the shelter they found the whole area ablaze – Bowhill & Hubbard's shoe factory was a mass of flames and blazing woodwork had fallen all round the shelter they had just vacated. The tarmac, sticky under their feet, clung warmly to their shoes. People were running, jumping over piles of bricks and then, to the girl, came the most terrible sight of the war. From out of the smoke in Heigham Street galloped a horse, his coat covered in a foam of fear, his eyes glazed with terror as he made his way up Old Palace Road and disappeared into the smoke.

The girl grabbed her mother's arm and declared they must get home. As they made their way they passed people crying in front of their shattered homes, with firemen, frustrated by lack of water because of damaged water-mains, helplessly standing by burning buildings. They saw heroic rescue workers risking their lives as they crawled into wrecked houses to drag out badly injured people and soldiers working endlessly wherever help was needed. When the girl and her mother reached home, they had a warm drink and sat quietly, thankful they were safe. It was not until the following day that they heard that a shelter near the Dolphin public house had received a direct hit killing 14 people. They realised that in the smoke and confusion they had missed taking refuge in this shelter when they had desperately been searching for cover a few hours before.

At the Norvic Dairy on Dereham Road – the only shop more or less intact for many streets around – owner and wife surveyed their shattered windows and the small queue of dishevelled customers standing by their door. With the same determination that had kept these small shops open throughout the war years, years in which their goods arrived in bulk and each small ration had to be carefully weighed, each tiny coupon cut from the ration books, and coupons by the thousand counted, they shook the dust from their coats, pushed what glass there was left from their windows and pulled their counter across to the open space and started serving, through the window-frame, the growing crowd on the pavement. They had been serving for some hours when an errand boy struggling along on his trade bicycle stopped. His basket was filled with daffodils which he had hoped to deliver to florists in the City but the path ahead being impassable he called to the grocer asking if he would like to sell them. The people waiting patiently for their rations turned to look at the clean bunches of flowers. Old ladies whose only possessions were the

torn clothes they stood up in, housewives clutching the only money that had survived, with no homes, and, at that moment, very little hope rushed to buy, just to clutch the daffodils in their grimy hands as the one symbol of beauty and sanity left to them.

Many people remember the Messenger Service, those young boys of between 16 and 18 who rode their bicycles, often on flat tyres, through streets thickly strewn with glass and debris as bombs rained down, constantly being thrown from their machines.

One of these boys, John Grix, was so keen to join he lied about his age and was only 15 on the night of these raids. He cycled two miles to duty through the heaviest bombed area, repeatedly jumping from his machine to lay flat as bombs whistled down and, when passing one building that was blazing furiously, his hands were sprayed with acid shooting from its windows into the street. On arrival at his centre he reported for duty and throughout the night he obeyed instructions which included travelling through devastated parts of the City to lead firemen from the County to the various reported incidents. The Messengers, unlike the other Civil Defence Services, did their work singly. Not until hours later did this boy mention that first aid was necessary for his acid-burnt hands, and after-

With the shortage of petrol and tyres, the bike came into its own during the war, as this picture of Bury Street shows.

wards, when daylight came, he volunteered to join parties of rescue workers. That night he slept at the Report Centre and the following day helped wherever he could in the City. When the siren again sounded he once more made many nightmare journeys during which he was blown from his machine five times. And this boy's story was not unique; many more of these young messengers performed tasks of unbelievable courage.

The homeless had to be seen to and outside the City Hall queues had begun to form as early as seven o'clock that morning. Most of the homeless had had their clothing destroyed and this was not easily replaced – an oddity of the Norwich raids was the high proportion of retail shops destroyed or damaged – so a centre for the distribution of clothing was opened on Cow Hill. Other essentials were the 8,000 registered customers who had to be re-registered and 14,000 emergency ration cards that had to be issued. Furniture from damaged homes had to be removed and storage found. Lost ration books and identity cards had to be replaced and grants for immediate financial help given. Temporary accommodation had to be found and missing relatives traced. All this work was undertaken by the staff of the local authority and the Assistance Board, some of whom had themselves suffered. When it is realized that the number of people affected ran into thousands the task must have been Herculean. As the survivors

began to be settled they remembered these nights: how 20 Church Army vans had served over 10,000 cups of tea during the raids; how six YMCA vans worked in relays reporting for duty while the bombs were still dropping; how the Salvation Army canteens also distributed cups of tea by the thousand. 400 meals were served on the Tuesday from the 11 Rest Centres established by the Education Authority and Welfare Services of the City.

The City of London sent a mobile unit staffed by experienced helpers who, with the knowledge gained in other blitzed towns, had set up a relief depot at the Model Senior Girls' School in Dereham Road. The unit comprised three travelling vans and marquees which could accommodate a hundred people. This unit also supplemented the issue of clothing and personal belongings.

Members of the WVS worked very hard: they served tea to casualties at the hospital, distributed large amounts of emergency clothing, supervised the removal of furniture from bombed houses, and staffed Rest homes.

MAGNA did a magnificent job in providing assistance and shelter for 400 of the homeless. Members went round the bombed areas advising, dealing with minor casualties, and often sheltering people in their own homes.

St Stephen's Street on the morning after the blitz.

Looking towards Orford Place. ▶

Looking towards St Stephen's Gates. ▶▶

The Morning After

On the morning after the blitz you wonder just what damage had been inflicted on the City and dressing hurriedly go out on to the streets to satisfy your curiosity. Here you meet small groups of people exchanging 'bomb stories', information, and rumours: 'Curl's is burnt out'; 'I hear Woolworth's has gone for a Burton'; 'St Benedict's had it very bad'; 'There's been a lot of people killed in the shelter in Chapel Field Gardens', and, ominously, 'They'll be back tonight.' You listen, smile, and walk on.

As you approach Chapel Field Gardens you see that the park is a shambles and you think 'They must have been right, people could not have survived this.' Later you learn that four 500 kg bombs fell on the park. One of them, an unexploded bomb, was confirmed by the Wardens' Service Reconnaissance Officers P Scott and W C Shore and was removed by the

Army Bomb Disposal Unit on 7 June.

You move along Chapel Field North towards Theatre Street. All around you windows have been blown out. The Christian Spiritualist Church and a number of fine old houses are severely damaged and at the end of the road Corporation lorries and fire-engines bar your way. Looking beyond them down Theatre Street, the Theatre Royal and E Pordage, the banana merchants, are still standing but look to be damaged.

As you walk down Chapel Field East small spirals of smoke rise from the charred wood you kick from your path. The chocolate factory of A J Caley is ringed by fire-tenders and lorries and the air is filled with the smell of smoke and burnt sugar. The factory's large windows are empty of glass and through these gaps the floors can be seen littered with ruined machinery – girders stand out at odd angles and a corrugated building has twisted itself in the heat and burst from its foundations. You continue along Chapel Field Road and as you approach the top of St Stephen's

Chocolate was in short supply anyway, and production at Caley's was not helped by the bombing!

Surveying the damage from Orford Place. ▶

Street you pass R W Roy's refreshment rooms, which had been damaged. Turning into narrow St Stephen's Street the full impact of the raid's damage lies before you. The Unicorn public house, Maypole Dairy, Leach's

The St Stephen's Street frontage of the Boar's Head.
▶▶

the oil and colour merchants, Stockings the butcher, Matthes the baker and Fieldings the cycle dealer are some of the first buildings you see to be damaged. The road is covered with tiles, broken glass, and bricks all of which slows your progress. At one point you stumble, and catch your breath, but it's all right, the figure at your feet is only a dummy fallen from a shop window.

As the damage becomes more severe you look up at the shop names; Elmo's stores, Wilson the costumiers, Tyler's the boot makers, and Peacock's Stores, the bazaar so loved by the City's children – both their shops are badly gutted and one is damaged beyond repair.

At the corner of Surrey Street the Boar's Head public house which has stood here since the 15th century has been gutted and its roof stands skeleton-like against the sky – gone is the picturesque thatch and the ancient timbered interior is destroyed. On the opposite corner the premises of Millett the clothier have also been laid waste and up the street you can see that the Norwich Union has been hit. Opposite the Boar's Head public house, Barwell's the wine merchants and Barclays Bank have sustained severe structural damage.

Your way is barred by a fireman who calls to you to go back, but as he turns away you go on climbing over criss-crossed hoses that litter the road. People are working all around you – salvaging, damping down smouldering wood, with men up ladders pulling away dangerous over-

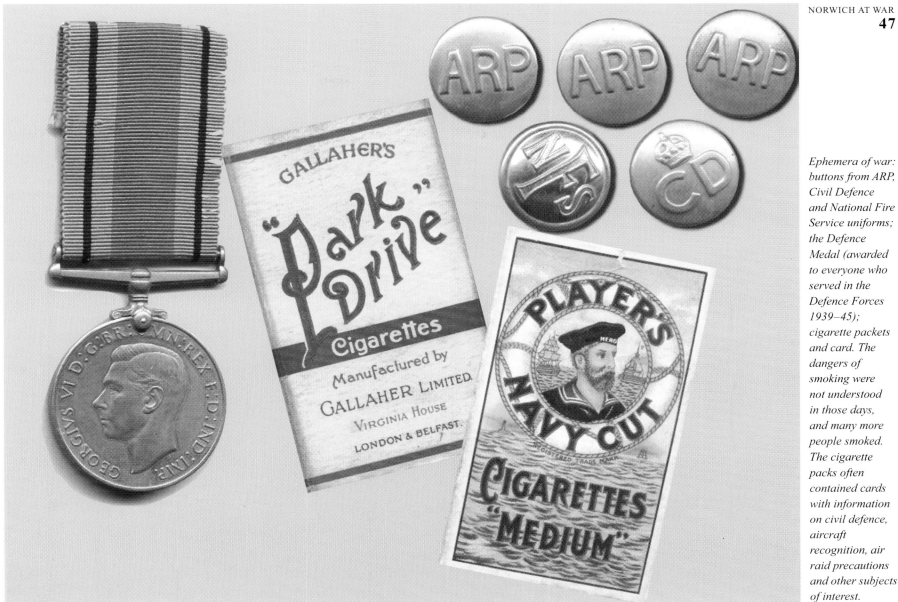

Ephemera of war: buttons from ARP, Civil Defence and National Fire Service uniforms; the Defence Medal (awarded to everyone who served in the Defence Forces 1939–45); cigarette packets and card. The dangers of smoking were not understood in those days, and many more people smoked. The cigarette packs often contained cards with information on civil defence, aircraft recognition, air raid precautions and other subjects of interest.

*Considerable
damage in
Rampant Horse
Street.*

hanging rubble, they take no notice of your presence and presume you have a right to be there.

At the corner of Rampant Horse Street Buntings the draper's large plate-glass windows lie in piles of fragmented glass. The shop is empty,

there are no counters, no millinery section, no showroom promenades, no main aisles, all have been destroyed.

Across the road the Saxone shoe shop has spilled itself out on to the pavement. Gordon Thoday, silk merchants, is an empty shell and Curl's,

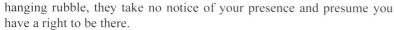

Scenes of devastation in Orford Place on the morning after the raid.

Miraculously, the new City Hall (like every other building of civic importance) escaped the devastating blitz. This view from the tower shows the damage to the Hippodrome and St Giles Street.

◄◄ *The show cannot go on: the Hippodrome Theatre, St Giles, damaged beyond theatrical traditions.*

◄ *Had this bomb, which destroyed the Clover Leaf Café on Guildhall Hill, been intended, as many people believed at the time, for the City Hall?*

one of the city's largest departmental stores, is just not there any more. All that is left is a mountain of brick rubble that stretches out across the road to join more debris that had once been the interior of Woolworth's. Fuller the chemist and Timpson's shoe shop are unrecognisable. The back of the Haymarket Theatre displays large jagged gaps open to the air. Boots the chemist, the Co-operative Insurance Society offices, Rosson's gun shop, Tacon & Cowells' seed shop, all are badly damaged. St Stephen's Church is also damaged but only slightly.

Through the gap that had once been Curl's you can see that Brigg Street has been devastated, with the premises of Pilch the sports outfitter, Sullivan the confectioner, Audrey the costumier, and Louis the hairdresser all torn apart. Through the same gap you also see Orford Place and here Samson's Army and Navy Stores, the club rooms of the Church of England Young Men's Society, and Curls' offices have all disappeared. The sight of this bomb damage in the heart of the City depresses you and turning you hurry away to Castle Meadow and hope returns, the Castle still stands defiantly on its mound, undamaged.

You almost run down Davey Steps and there before your eyes are the City Hall, the Guildhall, and the Church of St Peter Mancroft which, apart from slight damage, have survived. You cross the Market to St Giles Street and find that the Cloverleaf Café has sustained a direct hit and its

roof blocks the corner of Lower Goat Lane – a very near miss to the tower of the City Hall you think. The blast from this bomb has severely damaged the Raven public house, Gardiner & Lacey the chemists, and the London & Norwich Press. Further along the Hippodrome has received a direct hit from a high-explosive bomb which has completely demolished one wall and lifted the theatre stage into the air where it has settled down on its fallen supports, intact, and four inches above its normal level. The Black Horse public house and Swains the photographer have been damaged. Mr George Swain was himself to take many vivid photographs of the devastated City.

Further along St Giles Street there is some damage to Lacey & Lincoln the builders' merchants, the Salvation Army Citadel, Mortimer's Hotel, the Conservative Club, and the Norwich High School for Boys, but this is not of a severe nature.

Walking on, you reach the top of Grapes Hill and here the devastation is such that only a very large high-explosive bomb and a number of incendiaries could have caused it – the Grapes Hotel, the Midland Bank, and Yaxley's wireless shop are damaged beyond repair and Duff, Morgan & Vermont's garage has been gutted by fire. Later, at the top of the hill, the presence of a 500 kg unexploded bomb was confirmed by P Scott and W C Shore – this was removed by the Army Bomb Disposal Unit on 2 June.

You thread your way through the debris down Grapes Hill and here the sight before you is horrific. 21 houses on the west side of the hill are seriously damaged and the east side has not escaped. Pausing a while you see curtains flapping from smashed casement windows and the fractured external walls through which tangled, charred piles of furniture lie in rooms unrecognisable even to their owners, who stand in helpless bewilderment before them.

But it is at the junction of Grapes Hill and St Benedict's Street that your eyes for a few seconds cannot fully accept the scene. The area of St Benedict's Gates has been torn from its foundations – the whole cross-road section is one enormous crater – gone are the premises of Brett the antique furniture dealers, the 18th century posting tavern, the Fountain public house, Ashworth & Pike the bakers, the St Benedict's Post Office, Vittell's the grocers, Thirkettle the butcher and Hicks the fishmonger. Sec-

◀◀ *Looking up St Benedict's.*

◀ A disappointed regular surveys damage to his local – the Crown in St Benedict's Street.

tions of the City wall are intact but stand perilously near to the crater. St Benedict's Church, a fine example of the Early English style, has only one wall left standing, but the tower, apart from large holes torn in its side, is still standing.

You walk up St Benedict's Street towards the City and see further devastation. The Crown, the Stag, and the Cardinal's Cap public houses are severely damaged and some eight houses have been totally destroyed, and as far as the eye can see there is no glass in any window-frame. On the other side of the crater at the corner of Dereham Road and Barn Road the Barn Tavern is devastated, with the damage extending to Ketteringham the motor agents, the Regal Cinema and St Benedict's Garage – people stop to look at this scene with unbelieving eyes. Thinking you have seen enough for one day, you turn and walk home.

Over the weeks that follow there slowly unfolds a picture of the damage inflicted on the City.

Dereham Road Area

Dereham Road, from the crater at the corner of St Benedict's Street to near the Norwich Road, received many direct hits from the bombing. Norwich Cemetery was hit a number of times by 250 and 500 kg bombs – two of

these were later confirmed as unexploded bombs by Inspector Buttle, one of the Police Reconnaissance Officers, and were removed by the Army Bomb Disposal Unit – people at the time thought a cemetery was the best place for them to fall. Helena Road, where many gardens backed on to the Cemetery, not only suffered from the blast from these bombs but was also

The corner shop, Exeter Street, 'closed all hours' by a 500kg bomb.

An unexploded bomb badly damaged this house in Bond Street. The bomb was found in the garden.

hit by a further three 500 kg bombs which fell over the short area this road covers from Dereham Road to Stafford Street.

On his visit to Norwich after the blitz the Duke of Kent inspected this road where scarcely a house remained habitable and he spoke to a Mrs A M Allen who was searching the rubble of her home holding a basket containing items she had already retrieved. The Duke advised her with a kindly smile to leave this work to the demolition parties as the walls of her house wreck liable to collapse. Of the houses in this unhappy street most of them had lost their windows and many were beyond repair – chimney-pots had crashed through roofs, tiles had fallen, and gutters were torn from fractured walls.

On the Bowthorpe Road the Norwich Institution (later to be the West Norwich Hospital) had been badly damaged depriving the City of 600 non-casualty beds.

Bombs fell near Connaught Road and here many houses suffered, including I H Wilde's butcher shop. At the corner of Merton Road a 500 kg unexploded bomb was examined by Inspector Mitchell and removed by the Army Bomb Disposal Unit on 3 June. At the top of Bond Street a 500 kg unexploded bomb was confirmed by P Scott and Inspector Buttle. It was removed on 5 June and in the course of their inspection they found

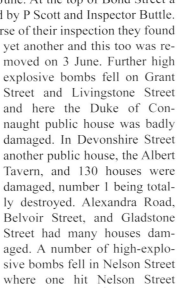

No 1, Merton Road, recorded in a photo by E C Le Grice. He recalled that a bomb fell in the front garden while the inmates and friends were sleeping in the cellar.

yet another and this too was removed on 3 June. Further high explosive bombs fell on Grant Street and Livingstone Street and here the Duke of Connaught public house was badly damaged. In Devonshire Street another public house, the Albert Tavern, and 130 houses were damaged, number 1 being totally destroyed. Alexandra Road, Belvoir Street, and Gladstone Street had many houses damaged. A number of high-explosive bombs fell in Nelson Street where one hit Nelson Street School which was a Rest Centre at the time. On Old Palace Road the Rainbow public house was

destroyed, and the premises of E W Adams, wholesale provision merchants, and A Arden, botanical brewers, were severely damaged.

On the corner of Old Palace Road and Dereham Road the Dial public house had been gutted and on the main Dereham Road Leveridge's the builders, the Model Senior Girls' School, the Lord John Russell public house, the Distillery public house, and the Robin Hood public house were all damaged. Dereham Road Baptist Church had its large window blown out, and its roof laid bare to the wind and weather.

An elderly lady living at 114 West End Street was on the night of the blitz sheltering in her larder under the stairs. Suddenly her house shuddered and there was a deep roaring sound as the door and walls of her larder collapsed about her. A large hole appeared at her feet. Shaken but unhurt she clambered round the hole and over the rubble to safety. The full miracle of her escape was not known until seven weeks later when it was found that the damage to the house had not been caused by blast as was at first thought but by a 500 kg unexploded bomb which had penetrated the roof, her bed, the bedroom floor and the larder ceiling, missing her by inches and burying itself eight feet beneath the larder floor. This incident is still remembered by Reconnaissance Officers as one of the most remarkable escapes in their records.

On Heigham Road St Philip's Church and the Stafford Arms public house were slightly damaged. Also affected were the premises of Howell & Turner the cabinet-makers, the Norwich Pattern Company and T

Daniels the wholesale confectioners. Two 500 kg bombs fell in Lothian Street destroying a number of private houses together with the Marquis of Lothian public house. The vibrating blast damaged a large number of houses in Orchard Street, including the shops of Mrs E R Brown and Mr G Howes and the Earl of Cardigan public house. Nearby, at the top of

Exeter Street, a 500 kg unexploded bomb was inspected and confirmed by P Scott and Inspector Buttle.

Earlham Road area

On College Road the Norwich Diocesan Training College was hit by showers of incendiary bombs and young girl students fought desperately to save the Main Hall and Chapel with stirrup pumps and buckets of water, but the task proved impossible and the building was destroyed.

Midland Street. This old property suffered from earth shock; a bomb had dropped 30 yards away.

Bombs have no respect for seats of learning: the Teachers' Training College, College Road.

High-explosive bombs fell on Edinburgh Road totally destroying two houses. Another fell on Winter Road and here, as well as houses, two shops were damaged, those of Mr Roe the baker and Mrs Coldham the grocer. Havelock Road and Mill Hill Road sustained a great deal of damage from blast and 7 West Parade was totally destroyed by a direct hit which damaged 18 other properties. On Henderson Road four houses were badly shattered and many more were damaged to varying degrees. A 500 kg bomb exploded in Paragon Street, the general damage was extensive but not severe, one of the business premises affected being Ketts' furniture depository.

At the other end of Earlham Road in Gipsy Lane a suspected unexploded bomb was confirmed by Inspector Doe, but at 8am on 30 April this exploded before the Army could defuse it.

A chance not to pay the gas bill as the British Gas Light Company stands in ruins at the corner of Heigham Road and Dereham Road.

An army of workmen repair water and gas mains. Life must go on at Caernarvon Road. ▶

Duff Morgan's garage, Earlham Road. It would not be hard to explain to customers why their repairs had not been carried out. ▶ ▶

One of the city's newest churches, St Anne's on the Earlham Estate, was destroyed and St Thomas's Church was gutted by fire.

St Thomas's, Earlham Road. Exposed to the heavens, at least the shell was preserved. ▶

This bomb fell during the blitz and buried itself 35 feet deep in Waterloo Park. It was removed a month later. ▶ ▶

Aylsham Road Area

One large bomb, reported to be of 1,000 kg calibre, fell near the corner of Drayton Road and St Martin's Road and another, this time of 500 kg fell by Green Hills Road where five houses were badly damaged.

In Wensum Park a 1,000 kg unexploded bomb found its way into the fishpond and after lying there undetected it exploded at 1am on 29 April.

Yet another brewery bombed. At least this section was manufacturing mineral water for Messrs Bullard's, St Miles Bridge, Coslany Street.

Rackham Road had 64 houses damaged, Stone Road had three houses totally destroyed and many others damaged. On Philadelphia Lane some of the places worst affected included St Luke's Mission Hall, the White Cottage public house, and the Prospect public house, while the Crawshay Arms public house and 145 houses were in need of repair.

Moving towards the City from Aylsham Road, at the corner of Waterloo Road St Augustine's Council Schools were hit by a 500 kg bomb and at Pitt Street two further bombs fell, one near St Martin's Lane, the other on the corner of St Mary's Plain where the Baptist Chapel was gutted by fire. An unexploded bomb was reported at the Heatrae Works, but this was discredited by Inspector Buttle. Steppings & Tungate's garage and the Flower-in-Hand public house in Pitt Street were among other properties damaged.

Heigham Street area

Pilgrims Hall, St Mary's Plain. Preserved from slum clearance and now nearly destroyed by bombs.

The Eagle Steam Laundry in Helford Street was badly shattered and seven houses were affected. The picturesque Dolphin public house was gutted by fire. This ancient building, which had once been the home of a bishop, was scarred and blackened but its main walls remained intact. Just past the Dolphin by the corner of Raynham Street a surface shelter received a direct hit which killed 14 people. Howhill & Hubbard's shoe factory in Heigham Street was also gutted by fire. A 500 kg bomb had fallen by the corner of Station Road and Heigham Street School, which had been turned into a British Restaurant, was destroyed. St Bartholomew's Church, Heigham, had its interior shattered and its bells, fallen from the

The north side of the nave in St Bartholomew's church. ▶

Westwick Street, after the blitz.
▶▶

tower, lay half covered by rubble alongside what was left of the font in an isle of heat-flaked stone pillars.

Westwick Street area

Coleman's Wincarnis Works were almost totally destroyed. The Corporation Depot lay in ruins and the loss of equipment and vehicles added greatly to the difficulties encountered by the City in its efforts to deal with blitz damage. Other victims were Hales' factory which had been taken over by Sexton Sons & Everard, A W Cushions' yard at Balbon Wharf, Twiddy's coach works, Utting's corn-mill, Bullard's old Mineral Water Factory, and the Marsham Tyre Company. Nearby the Midland & Great Northern Joint Railway's City Station was destroyed by some of the many bombs that fell in this area.

More problems as the Corporation Depot, Westwick Street, loses all its equipment. ▶

Bomb damage at City railway station. ▶▶

Oak Street area

Along much-battered Oak Street the Buck public house had been totally destroyed. This old pub had an interesting connection with an ancient charity which each year dispensed clothing to the needy. In Oak Street the St Martin at Oak Mission Hall and the old

Empire Picture House were badly damaged; the latter was being used for the storage of sugar. Another public house, this time the White Lion, sustained further damage and all the little yards that lead from this street were hit. Angel Yard was completely gutted by fire, Little Buck Yard, Bath House Yard, Royal Oak Yard, Old Brew Yard, and Swan Yard were all torn and battered, and here it wasn't only bricks and mortar and lives we lost, but a wealth of our history. At nearby Gildencroft the Friends' Meeting House was destroyed. This building, which dated back to 1699, had been associated with many famous people and Elizabeth Fry, Amelia Opie, and Joseph Gurney lay in its adjoining burial ground.

Drayton Road area

Twelve 500 kg bombs were recorded as having fallen along Drayton Road and in Valpy Avenue and at Wheeler Road four houses were destroyed

and many damaged. Edwards & Holmes' shoe factory was destroyed. At Stone Road three houses were destroyed and others damaged. An unexploded bomb was reported at Slough Bottom off Drayton Road and this was confirmed by Inspector Buttle. It was removed by the Army Bomb Disposal Unit on 7 June. At Junction Road nine houses were totally destroyed, five badly wrecked, and 74 others classified as damaged. This damage had been caused by a 1,000 kg bomb which had made a very large crater and had tossed huge masses of clay through the roofs of numbers 91 and 93, which were mistaken for unexploded bombs.

Magdalen Street area

A 250 kg bomb fell in the grounds of the Blind Institution in Magdalen Street and also damaged a nearby Police Station. St Paul's Mission Room together with some 35 houses on the west side of Magdalen Road were left usable if somewhat battered.

The Congregational Church Sunday School on Clarke Road received a direct hit. Blast inflicted damage in Starling Road, Magpie Road, and St George Street in the latter the Golden Can public house was destroyed.

In Calvert Street a row of seventeenth century three-storeyed gable-ended houses were shattered beyond repair, and Cottage number 1 at Doughty's Hospital was also damaged. Most of the destruction in this area was caused by 500 kg high-explosive bombs.

A bomb in Barrack Street partly destroyed the Horse Barracks public house and damaged Williams' tannery, the Marquis of Granby public house and the premises of Royall the newsagent and Brown the butcher.

Oak Street: servicemen clearing away debris after the blitz. Inset: the hole in the roof was caused by the attic window falling intact. An unexploded bomb was suspected.

The Horse Barracks public house, Barrack Street.

Mile Cross area

▶▶ *A 1000kg unexploded bomb crashed through this roof in Angel Road. It was later removed by the Bomb Disposal Squad.*

8 Margaret Paston Avenue, the work of a 50kg bomb. ▶

Many 500 kg bombs were logged as having fallen on the Mile Cross Estate. On Le Froy Road 11 houses were damaged and on Rye Avenue one house was so severely damaged that it had to be demolished. Burgess Road had two houses destroyed and 48 damaged, while Oxnead Road had three houses badly damaged and many slightly affected. Hansard Road had one very badly damaged house. Appleyard Crescent suffered varying degrees of damage to 124 houses and Mile Cross Road had 77 properties badly damaged with a further 23 slightly so.

On Woodcock Road, near the Mile Cross Estate, the Hill House Dairy and another 136 houses were damaged

▶▶ *A 1000kg unexploded bomb was found in the passage of 15/17 Angel Road.*

The bomb fell in a heavy gale and the occupant of 46 Oxnead Road did not even hear the explosion. ▶

Hellesdon area

A stock of bombs, presumably off target, fell in the vicinity of Hellesdon Hall Road, behind the Church of St Mary the Virgin, and in nearby fields. Further east round the boundary road a 500 kg bomb fell at the corner of Mile Cross Lane, and on Catton Grove Road explosions damaged the premises of Mrs Newman the confectioner and postmistress, Charles Harris the grocer, Howard Ganderton the butcher, Charles Brightman the fish-frier, and De Carle the chemist.

St Clement's Hill area

On St Clement's Hill the Blyth Secondary School received damage to its cookery classroom in Clare House. Cycle-sheds and the doors and windows of other school buildings were also affected by blast. Marionville Cottages, Lime Works Cottages, and the Henry Attoe lime works fell victim to a group of 500 kg bombs that were scattered over this area.

◄◄ *This substantial crater was in Dakin Road.*

◄ *Rupert Street after the April 1942 blitz. Small businesses and private houses are ripped apart.*

On Chamberlin Road 24 houses were damaged, as were 56 in Afghan Place. In Pelham Road nine houses were damaged beyond repair and Rosebery Road had 50 houses damaged or destroyed. Dakin Road had four houses destroyed, Millers Lane five, Elm Grove Lane two, and all had numerous properties damaged.

Damage to properties was usually caused by blast and usually affected such things as window-frames, chimney-pots, tiles, sashes and ceilings. The word 'damage' which is here used so often to describe the condition of properties after a raid does not take into account the effect it had on the occupants, and particularly the distressed housewives. It does not describe the soot which poured down the chimney in great clouds and covered everything and it does not describe the housewife's frustration on finding the water-supply cut off, robbing her of the means to clean up. The soot was, of course, everywhere: in the clothes in the wardrobe, in the sheets and blankets, ingrained in the curtains which blew through empty window-frames, in the food in the pantry – in fact you yourself smelt of soot, it was in your clothes and in your hair.

Rupert Street area

Once again the bombing was to cause immense damage in the confined narrow streets of this area. In Rupert Street itself among the many properties damaged in varying degrees were the International Stores,

the premises of Hurns the blind-makers, Newby the pork butcher, Miss Joan Mackley the ladies' hairdresser and Pestell the baker, and the Black Eagle and Norfolk Tavern public houses. Off Rupert Street all four houses in Eagle Passage were completely destroyed. At Albert Buildings, Wellington Terrace, Ellwood's Buildings, and Bixfields Buildings the

Rupert Street was hit on more than one occasion. This scene speaks for itself.

damage was so severe that many of the surviving properties had to be demolished.

Vauxhall Street was not so badly affected but even so 11 houses were badly damaged, ten houses had later to be demolished, and 54 others were affected by blast.

Union Street. Here a Church Army Hall, two blocks of flats and the John Bull public house sustained bomb damage.

Union Place, Manchester Street: devastated.

Manchester Street. Here five houses were destroyed, four had to be evacuated, and eight others were demolished at a later date.

Somerleyton Street. The Somerleyton public house and its adjoining buildings were destroyed. 21 houses had to be declared 'unsafe', three remained habitable but in a bad state, three had to be evacuated while repairs were made, and 32 other properties were damaged.

Essex Street. Here 171 houses were damaged and four houses and the Curriers' Arms public house destroyed. 13 of the damaged houses needed to be demolished. The slightly damaged properties included the Royal Oak and the George the Fourth public houses.

Kings Square. All 17 houses in the Square were so badly damaged that they had to be demolished.

Greave's Buildings. A 500 kg bomb destroyed four houses.

Globe Street. The Globe public house was severely damaged and four houses were destroyed. A further eight houses and a workshop were so badly shaken they had to be pulled down. At Globe Row and Reads Buildings a total of seven houses were destroyed and others damaged.

Salford Street. Among the many properties damaged was the William the Fourth public house.

Chapel Street. Two houses were completely destroyed, the Duke of Wellington public house sustained heavy damage, and the Trinity Mission Hall had its windows blown out and lost its chimney-pots.

Rosary Road area

Ethel Road. A 500 kg bomb destroyed four houses, while on Ella Road another 500 kg bomb scored a direct hit on one house and blast damaged 13 other properties.

Rosary Road. The Goodyear Tyre depot, the King's Arms public house, Robinson's Garage, the Evening Gun public house, the Norwich Gas Works Social and Recreation Club, the buildings at the old football ground (the 'Nest'), the Superintendent's house at the Rosary Cemetery, and St Matthew's Church sustained varying degrees of damage.

St Leonard's Road. Bombs destroyed five houses and damaged Thorpe Hamlet School and many other properties.

All Saints' Green area

Along Surrey Street the premises of the Norwich Union Insurance Societies suffered severe damage. The German High Command in their reports described the Norwich air raids of April 1942 as reprisals. The Times spoke of these raids as having caused damage in many parts of the City and this news was to travel far and wide across the world. The Norwich Union, the world-famous insurance company, was overwhelmed by the enquiries they received, not only from the British Isles but by telegraph from Baghdad, Buenos Aires, Cape Town, Haiti, Kingston, Lisbon, New York, Sydney and Tenerife. These must all have been warmly appreciated.

The Fire Office block received a direct hit on the Monday night. One section collapsed leaving gaping holes in walls and ceilings in rooms where the formerly well-kept records were now in complete disorder. The bombed-out Fire Office staff was offered accommodation in the Life

Office premises and within a few days 150 were rehoused and had resumed work. On the Wednesday night incendiary bombs fell and set fire to the Stationery Store. Despite the efforts of the Norwich Union's own fireguards the fire spread through the warehouse and the adjacent buildings.

Fortunately these buildings were detached so the damage did not extend beyond the store. One great loss was the carefully arranged stock of paper, forms, envelopes, etc, which in the prevailing conditions were almost irreplaceable. But in a few hectic weeks additional supplies were secured and the department was again functioning in accommodation placed at its disposal by the Life Society. The burnt-out Stationery Store had previously been known as the 'Victoria Hall' and had been taken over by the Norwich Union in 1920. Older people remembered it as a picture palace where you could gain entrance on the production of a jam jar if you did not have the price of admission.

In Surrey Street the Bus Station was again hit.

At the Carlton Theatre in All Saints' Green a 1,000 kg bomb fell through the side of the building. The damage was thought at the time to have been caused by blast. It was not until several days later, and after some hundreds of people had visited the cinema, that a huge bomb was detected and inspected by C W Shore and Inspector Buttle. It was removed by the Army Bomb Disposal Unit and a Clearance Certificate was issued by them on 4 May. The citizens of Norwich had sat through Robert Young's performance in *Louisiana Purchase* blissfully unaware that at any moment the building could have blown up. In this confined area, and bearing in mind the size of the bomb, casualties would undoubtedly have been very heavy.

On Timber Hill two 250 kg bombs fell in Mouncer's Yard damaging the Strict Baptist Chapel and a number of shops including the fish shop of Valori Bros. In Ber Street bombs fell opposite Bonds' Garage and behind the King's Arms public house. Off Ber Street, Horns Lane School was hit and the Bartholomew Tavern in Thorn Lane was damaged.

It has proved impossible to give a comprehensive account of the effects of the 'Baedeker raids' – the 'blitz' – on Norwich. So many incendiary bombs fell it is impossible for them all to be recorded and enemy aircraft, apart from bombing, also strafed streets and buildings with machine-gun fire, while the shrapnel from our own anti-aircraft guns added to the overall destruction. The above then is a record of some of the bombs which fell on the nights of 27 and 29 April 1942.

Lady fire-watchers on the roof of a large shop in Orford Place.

Fortunately, before the blitz, Bomb Reconnaissance courses held at Bury St Edmunds were attended by members of the Police Force and the ARP. The accurate reporting of the location of unexploded bombs helped in evacuation and traffic diversions and, even more importantly, they prevented the sending of Bomb Disposal Units on unnecessary journeys. Since the slightest vibration could detonate unexploded bombs the task of the Reconnaissance officers was not an easy one. The people's idea of ARP wardens as 'put that light out' busybodies was a little unkind to this highly organized and efficient body of men and women. From among their ranks many were to take the Bomb Reconnaissance course at Bury St Edmunds, including C W Shore, an ex-Royal Navy Gunnery Petty Officer whose knowledge of explosives was to

◄◄
Carlton Cinema, All Saints Green. A 1000kg unexploded bomb penetrated the outer wall. The cinema reopened for a number of days before discovery.

▶

Wardens proudly display their Scammel Pump.

▶▶

Joining the Auxiliary Territorial Service – the ATS – was one of the ways women could support the war effort.

▶

s an intelligent woman you know very well that we shall not win this war without using every weapon we possess — and *you* are one of these weapons! Man-power is not enough . . . we shall need every ounce of woman-power too, to defeat Hitler, and your energy, brains and enthusiasm will be used to the best advantage in the Auxiliary Territorial Service.

You can carry on your own job, or learn special work. The A.T.S. offers you valuable training, new friendships, change of scene, in fact an adventure into a new life! If you are aged between 17½ and 43 (parents' consent is necessary for those under 18) or an Ex-Service woman up to 50, there is a place for you and you will be used immediately.

When you enrol in the A.T.S. you will be asked to say what

Mutual Assistance: Services rendered to Norwich

Night of Monday/Tuesday, 27/28 April 1942

	Rescue Party	Ambulance	First Aid	SUC Party	Other Services
Acle	–	2	1	1	
American Ambulance	–	4	3	–	
Aylsham	1	2	1	1	
Blofield	–	1	1	1	
Bury St Edmunds	1	–	–	–	
Cambridge	6	6	3	–	
East Suffolk	1	–	–	–	
Great Yarmouth	3	3	–	5	
Hertfordshire	5	–	–	3	
Hickling	–	1	1	1	
Hoveton	–	1	1	1	
Ipswich	2	–	–	–	
North Walsham	1	2	1	1	
Royal Air Force	–	1	–	–	Fire convoy 30 cwt lorry 12 stretcher bearers
Southend	5	–	–	3	
Thorpe	1	1	1	1	
West Suffolk	2	–	–	–	

	Rescue Party	Ambulance	First Aid	SUC Party	Other Services
Acle	–	1	1	1	
Attleborough	1	–	–	–	
Aylsham	–	1	1	1	
Bedford	2	–	–	–	
Bishop's Stortford	3	–	–	–	
Blofield	–	1	1	1	
Brentwood	1	–	–	–	
Braintree	2	–	–	–	
Brightlingsea	1	–	–	–	
Burlingham	1	–	–	–	
Cambridge	3	3	–	–	Mr Lee Warner's Flying Squad
Chelmsford	1	–	–	2	
Colchester	6	–	–	3	
Coltishall	–	1	1	1	
Costessey	1	–	–	–	
Dereham	1	–	–	–	
Dunstable	–	–	–	1	
Great Yarmouth	3	3	–	4	2 officers
Hertfordshire	3	–	–	3	
Hoddeson	–	–	–	1	
Hoveton	–	1	1	1	

	Rescue Party	Ambulance	First Aid	SUC Party	Other Services
Letchwood	1	–	–	–	
Letchworth	–	–	–	1	
Luton	4	–	–	–	
North Walsham	–	1	1	1	
Reepham	1	1	1	1	
St Albans	1	–	–	–	
Southend	4	–	–	–	2 conducting officers, 1 dispatch rider
Sprowston	1	3	1	1	
Stanway	1	–	–	–	
Thorpe	–	3	1	2	
Watford	2	–	–	–	

be invaluable and whose work during these raids was to win him the British Empire Medal, and P Scott, the Assistant Chief Warden.

On the nights of 27 and 29 April 2942 many reports of unexploded bombs poured into the Report Centre. By daybreak 30 had been reported to Police Headquarters where they were dealt with by Inspectors Doe, Mitchell, and Buttle, and Sergeant Kemp.

Of the number of suspected unexploded bombs (UXBs) reported in the blitz 68 were confirmed by Reconnaissance Officers, 21 were diagnosed as exploded 50 kg bombs, and six were discredited for other reasons. Of the other reported unexploded bombs five exploded and the remainder were removed by the Army Bomb Disposal Squad.

Raid 30

1 May 1942 (Friday) Alert 01.35 hours

This was a night of fires when the main shopping centre of Norwich was nearly gutted. The raid began with several enemy aircraft challenging the City's ground defences. The challenge failed, with one exception. The single plane that did manage to penetrate the barrage dropped an E-type container which, on opening, scattered 700 explosive incendiary bombs along Heigham Street, across Duke Street, St Andrew Street, and the back of London Street.

In Heigham Street several fires broke out in premises already affected by previous raids. Fires also occurred in Oak Street, at the Norwich Corporation Electricity Works in Duke Street, the Free Library on the corner of Duke Street and St Andrew Street, Harmer's clothing factory in St Andrew Street, and Trevor Page's premises in Exchange Street. Fire also broke out at the rear of Garlands in London Street; this was contained by wardens and fireguards until the arrival of members of the National Fire Service who, with their more sophisticated apparatus, quickly extinguished the blaze.

All through this raid a strong wind was blowing and any one of these fires could easily have reached major proportions.

An impressive doorway and once the entrance to Messrs Harmers, St Andrew Street.

This month there was much praise for the efficiency of the Anderson and Morrison shelters which had saved the lives of hundreds of people during the air raids. As people emerged from these shelters each morning, with stiff limbs and dirty faces, they could still laugh. They laughed at two window-cleaners who, surveying the many shattered windows, shouted to a passing newspaperman, 'Hey bor, can you find us a job 'awkin' papers? It looks as if we'll be a signing on labour in the morning.'

They laughed at the tale of old Mrs Manclarke of Muspole Street who celebrated her one hundred and first birthday during this week. At the height of the main raid she refused brandy saying, 'I'm a life-long teetotaller and don't feel the necessity to break the habit.'

And there was the North countryman plane-spotter, new at the job. He was sent up on the factory roof and for a few minutes he looked and listened with anguished concentration, then he rushed to the telephone and shouted: 'Stop t'ruddy machinery, I can't hear a damn thing.'

Even at the height of the raids there was always something that could be laughed at, and this laughter helped immensely.

Raid 31

9 May 1942 (Saturday) Alert 00.38 hours

In this raid an intensive barrage of anti-aircraft gunfire was kept up for about an hour. Only one plane managed to penetrate these defences and it dropped two high-explosive bombs on the City. Both bombs fell on the boiler-house of the Woodlands Hospital (now the West Norwich Hospital) and caused considerable damage but, fortunately, there were no casualties. From fragments of these bombs which were examined after the raid it was judged that they were of the 1,000 kg calibre.

The rest of the raiders, unable to drop their bomb-loads on the City, made abortive attacks on the surrounding areas and dropped a large number of high-explosive bombs to the south-west and north-west of the City and thousands of incendiaries hit the Stoke Holy Cross and Poringland district causing numerous fires. Many delayed-action bombs were dropped and some of these exploded during the following days. One Junkers 88 was shot down in the Shotesham area.

It was thought that the first enemy aircraft to approach the City was

◄◄ Part of Woodlands Hospital (later the West Norwich Hospital).

◄ A riverside skeleton. Water continues to damp down the fire as the cathedral stands in the background unscathed.

being chased by an RAF fighter and because of this unwelcome attention it dropped its marker-flares, which had been intended for Norwich, over the Poringland area and following planes bombed on the flares.

The All Clear sounded at twenty minutes past two.

Raid 32

27 June 1942 (Saturday) Alert 02.05 hours

Almost a full moon shone down on the City, a light breeze blew from the east, and the barrage balloons slowly rose into the sky. To the northwest a far more brilliant light than that of the moon suddenly illuminated the City as parachute-flares ignited and slowly drifted to the ground. At this point anti-aircraft guns opened up but a number of enemy planes penetrated the defences and showered an estimated 20,000 incendiaries and some 33 high-explosive bombs on to the City.

Numerous fires were started, many reaching major proportions, but because of the comparatively small number of high-explosive bombs dropped, this raid was less terrifying than some earlier ones. An estimated 117 private houses were gutted and 246 were damaged. Many shops and offices suffered with 30 totally destroyed and ten others damaged by fire. Public buildings, schools, and churches also suffered with 21 gutted and 15 partially damaged. 29 factories and workshops were also destroyed, while four others were saved but extensively damaged.

The heroines of this raid must surely have been the grimy, dishevelled nurses at the Norfolk & Norwich Hospital. Wet from fire-hoses and with the hospital ringed by fires, they moved the

Clearing up in the Grove Road area, after Raid 32.

Considerable damage at the Norfolk and Norwich Hospital.

patients from the cellars to the grounds where ambulances and coaches eventually took them to another hospital a few miles away. The hospital itself, completely straddled by bombs, escaped serious damage, and although the operating theatre was destroyed most of its valuable equipment was saved.

It was on this night that Norwich could so easily have lost its most famous landmark, the Cathedral. Built, the history books tell us, at the

Damage in the Cathedral Close could have been much worse but for prompt action to control fires caused by incendiary bombs.

instigation of Bishop Herbert de Losinga, enlarged and added to over the years by succeeding Bishops to achieve its present grandeur, these books don't tell us of the gnarled fingers of the stone-carvers and the hundreds of other artisans that, ant-like, created this magnificent shrine and dedicated it to the Holy and Undivided Trinity. That night the hands of a German airman, curved round a lever, could in seconds have destroyed the work of centuries as 1,000 incendiaries fell within the precincts of The Close. Some 500 incendiaries fell to earth still held in the two containers which had failed to open, nevertheless 61 fell on the Cathedral and 36 more in an unopened container penetrated the transept roof – of these, 19 fell on hard ground surfaces or failed to ignite, the remainder causing eight fires in roofs and triforium.

The Close was well prepared with a Fire Protection Scheme that had been formulated by Mr A B Whittingham, the Surveyor to the Cathedral. On duty that night he was able to help his force in the task of extinguishing many of the incendiaries. There were three fire-watching posts; two in solicitors' offices in The Close and the third within the Cathedral at main roof-level.

The Cathedral had been made as fireproof as possible. All windows in the spire and most of those in the tower had been blocked up to prevent the tower from acting as a flue. Parapet walls, five feet high, had been constructed in the triforium arches to prevent fire spreading down to the organ and stalls. The incendiaries that fell on the north and south transepts near the tower set fire to the main supporting timbers, melting the lead covering and starting a blaze that could so easily have spread but for the prompt action of two solicitors' clerks and an unknown member of the Home Guard. The clerks, Mr E F Scales and Mr K E Webster, climbed to the Cathedral roof. On arrival the buckets of water they had so hopefully carried with them were found to be empty so with the help of more of the Cathedral's Fire Protection people they lowered a rope and pulled a fire-hose up to the blaze and eventually brought it under control. 40 incendiaries resulted in 11 more fires in The Close. Three of these fires were serious: numbers 63 and 66, once part of the twelfth-century infirmary, were completely destroyed and number 68 lost its top storey. Four other houses, numbers 51, 67, 71 and 75 suffered outbreaks of fire but these were dealt with successfully.

That venerable seat of learning the King Edward VI School had incendiary bombs fall on its science building, playground arcade, and lodge. The lodge was a total loss and the damage would have been much more

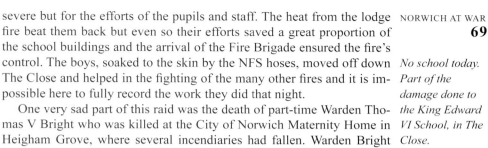

severe but for the efforts of the pupils and staff. The heat from the lodge fire beat them back but even so their efforts saved a great proportion of the school buildings and the arrival of the Fire Brigade ensured the fire's control. The boys, soaked to the skin by the NFS hoses, moved off down The Close and helped in the fighting of the many other fires and it is impossible here to fully record the work they did that night.

One very sad part of this raid was the death of part-time Warden Thomas V Bright who was killed at the City of Norwich Maternity Home in Heigham Grove, where several incendiaries had fallen. Warden Bright had run round to the front of the building to deal with the firebombs when a high-explosive bomb fell and he was buried under the debris of the building.

A regrettable loss to the City this night was the old-established family

No school today. Part of the damage done to the King Edward VI School, in The Close.

The view from the Castle Mound on the morning of 28 June 1942. In the centre of the skyline can be seen a barrage balloon, and in the left of the foreground is the entrance to one of the air-raid shelters that were built on the Cattle Market. In the centre of Farmers Avenue is the ruin of the Jolly Farmers, which had been burnt out the night before.

draper's shop of R H Bond & Sons Ltd, at All Saints' Green. This store incorporated within its structure the old Thatched Theatre – the home of photo plays, high-class variety, and dances of a previous era. The upper storey was used as a restaurant and the lower floor for the storage of furni-

ture. Now Bond's, with its arcades of elegant dresses, panel-wood aisles, and tall glass cabinets with their displays of fine bone china, was reduced to a burnt-out shell. Mrs B Jackson, an employee for many years, remembers the morning after the raid as she stood with a group of management and staff before the ruins. A Norwich housewife, ever hopeful, came up to them to ask when the salvage sales would be held. One of the Directors turned in rage and despair and said, 'Madam, there is not enough left to have a sale with.' The tone of this voice reflected the helplessness they all felt. They had no stock, no typewriters, no cash-tills. Those precious clothing coupons, so carefully counted, were in the strong-room which was inaccessible because ten days were to pass before the building was cool enough to enter.

One thing the fire did not destroy was the loyalty of the staff. They gathered round their employers and from the chaos was born improvisation. Buses were hired, parked in the car park, and used as shops. An old corrugated-iron building that had survived the flames became a restaurant, tea was brewed on an oil-stove, pastries were made and taken down Ber Street to E J Taylor, the baker, who baked them. A building opposite

◄◄ *Many Norwich shops were quick to improvise and carry on business as usual. In this case Bond's sold goods from disused buses.*

the burnt-out store on All Saints' Green was taken over to provide office accommodation and premises in Red Lion Street (now Barclays Bank) became their new store. The pawnbroker's shop on the corner of the bombed store was used as a retail outlet after its unredeemed stock had been sold from stalls erected nearby. At a later date some of the surviving structure was rebuilt and Bond's was once again in business.

◄ The destroyed Hebrew Synagogue.

◄ The masters must have been horrified, the boys delighted, to enjoy their enforced holiday. Bracondale School 1942.

◄◄ No rest in peace as St Mark's, City ROad, miraculously escapes a near miss.

Because of the number of bombs that fell that night it is not possible to record each incident but the following list gives some idea of the area of the City involved.

Armes Street (rear of number 81)	500 kg	
Barkers Street (Numbers 8,12)	250 kg	
Ber Street (Brooks Flats)	250 kg	Extensive damage
Ber Street (St Michael at Thorn church)		Gutted by fire
Bracondale Junior School	250 kg	
Carrow Abbey (in grounds)	250 kg	Blast damage
Cinder Ovens Row	250 kg	Ten houses demolished
Cotman Road (Number 16)	250 kg	Demolished
Dereham Road (Number 163)	500 kg	
Goldsmith Street	250 kg	
Hall Road (St Mark's church)	250 kg	
Harvey Lane (three houses past Morrison Lodge public house)		
Hatton Road	250 kg	
Heathside Road	250 kg	Blaze damage
Junction Road (Numbers 83–93)	1,000 kg	
Knox Road (Prison)	250 kg	Direct hit on prison wall
Marston Lane (field)	250 kg	Large crater
Mousehold (near Barracks)	250 kg	Crater
Oak Street (St Michael at Coslany church)		Roof damaged
Quebec Road (Waterworks)	250 kg	Crater
Riverside (north river-bank)	250 kg	Damage to warehouse
Rosary Road (Rosary Cemetery)	250 kg	Lodge demolished
St Julian's alley (St Julian's church)	250 kg	Church demolished
St Paul's Square (St Paul's church)		Gutted by fire
Spitalfields (Numbers 39–41)	250 kg	Two houses demolished
Standley Road	250 kg	Crater in road
Synagogue Street (Jewish Synagogue)		Gutted by fire
Telegraph Lane (Hillcrest)	250 kg	Large crater in road
Thorpe Road (Thorpe Station goods yard)	250 kg	Damage to goods shed
Unthank Road (Number 40)	250 kg	
Vincent Road (Numbers 4–6)	250 kg	Two houses demolished and five fatalities

The following sustained some damage, mostly caused by incendiaries:
All Saints' Green (Bond's); Anchor Street; Beaconsfield Road (No. 71); Ber Street (Windmill public house; Levine, draper); Berners Street;

Soldiers pause in their endless task of clearing up Bethel Street.

Bethel Street (Bethel Hospital; Norwich Labour Club and two houses); Bluebell Road; Botolph Street (Chamberlins, wholesale clothiers); Bullard Road; Bury Street (Nos. 22, 33); Calvert Street (Doughty's Hospital, the library); Camp Road; Carrow Hill (School); Carrow Road (Norwich City Football Club Ground); Chapel Field Gardens; Churchill Road; City Road (Lakenham Terrace, Young's builders); Colegate; Colman Road (No. 43); Corton Road (No. 3); Duke Street (St Mary's Baptist Chapel); Earlham Road (No. 85 and St Thomas's

Church); Eaton Park; Edinburgh Road (No. 8); Gipsy Lane (No. 138); Gordon Road (No. 24); Grove Avenue (No. 36); Grove Walk (St Albans Church); Hall Road (St Mark's Infants' School); Hatton Road (St Mark's Senior School); Harvey Lane (No.31); Hawes Place; Heigham Grove (City of Norwich Maternity Home); Heigham Street (School); Helena Road; Hilary Avenue; Horns Lane (School); Ipswich Grove; Ipswich Road (Tuckswood Farm, Harford Farm,

◄◄ *Yet another Anderson shelter intact after a house collapses around it in Trafford Road.*

◄ *A large lump of clay thrown from the crater made UXB officers suspect an unexploded bomb at this incident on Junction Road.*

Southwell Lodge); King Street (Morgan's Brewery); Kingsley Road; Knowsley Road; Long John Hill; Lloyd Road; Lothian Street; Magdalen Street; Marion Road; Market Place (City Hall); Martineau Lane (Railway bridge); Mountergate (bonded warehouse next to Ives's premises and near Synagogue Street); Muriel Road (No. 89); Muspole Street (Witton's boot factory); Oak Street (Church of St Martin-at-Oak); Palace Street (near King Edward VI Grammar School); Pilling Park Road (in woods); Plumstead Road (Nos. 29, 74 and top of Ketts Hill); Queen's Road (coal-yard and the Co-operative Wholesale Society Bakery yard); Recorder Road (Porters' timber yard); Rupert Street (No. 155); St George Street (Heatrae

◄◄ *The shell of the Trafford Arms in Grove Road.*

Works); St Giles Street (Ketts furniture store); St Leonard's Road (Thorpe Hamlet School); St Matthew's Road; St Philip's Road; St Stephen's Street (Thirkettle, provision dealer); Sandringham Road (No. 146 and rear of Denmark Arms public house); Southwell Road (Salvation Army Mission Room); Spencer Street; Surrey Street (near Millett's clothiers); Thorn Lane; Thorpe Road (Thorpe Station Goods Department, Red Cross Hut); Tombland (Harvey's Shop); Town Close Road (No. 1); Trafford Road (Nos. 17, 19, 37, 82 and the Trafford Arms public house); Trory Street; Unthank Road (Jenny Lind Hospital for Children); Victoria Street (No. 15); Vincent Road; WellesleyAvenue (No. 2); West Parade (No. 2); Wood Street (No. 15).

This raid only lasted three-quarters of an hour, but during its course many people were killed and maimed and much property destroyed.

Raid 33

28 July 1942 (Tuesday) Alert 01.20 hours

Several enemy aircraft were flying in the vicinity of the City when one of them swooped below the balloon barrage and coming in from the south flew across in a northerly direction. This plane dropped one 1,000 kg bomb and two Flam 500s containing incendiaries.

The 1,000 kg high-explosive bomb screamed down and fell to the rear of Trafford Road and Rowington Road where it penetrated deeply, exploded, and made a crater some 90 feet across. There were no casualties and the damage caused to the surrounding property was remarkably light considering the size of the bomb. Approaching the tall tower of the City Hall the container carrying incendiaries tumbled out from the bomb-bay of the aircraft and scattered its contents in practically a straight line causing fires in the premises of the Corporation Stores public house and Bagshaw's scrap-metal merchants in Oak Street; Bullard's Brewery in Westwick Street; Brett's furniture shop in St Benedict's Street; Keir Hardie Memorial Hall and two houses in St Gregory's Alley; George's leather factory, Pottergate, and Friends' First Day Schools in Pottergate. There was some further damage to houses in Sigismund Road, Mill Close, Southwell Road, Eleanor Road, Lanchester Court, Aurania Avenue, Pipe Burners' Yard, Essex Street, St Alban's Court, Lady Mary Road.

Several Heinkel 111s were involved in this raid and one struck the cable of a barrage balloon but continued on its course apparently undamaged.

The children this week heard the good news that the sweet ration was to be increased at the end of the month, while the adults were being urged to eat more potatoes and less bread so as to conserve wheat supplies which mainly had to be brought in by sea.

An amazing sight was to be witnessed at Carrow Road this week. The Americans were staging a baseball match between the Wildcats and the Cheyenne Broncs. This was to encourage friendly relations.

It was on 4 July 1942 that six American A-20 Boston light bombers flew out from Swanton Morley Airfield. This was the first offensive by a small band of Americans, the forerunners of the 8th Air Force which was to take over nearly 100,000 acres of Norfolk land for airfields within the next few months in such places as Shipdham, Hardwick, Snetterton Heath, Bodney, Hethel, Wendling, Tibbenham, Deopham Green, Seething, Old Buckenham, Horsham St Faiths, Rackheath and North Pickenham. The noise of aircraft engines being tested on the ground filled the ears of the people of Norfolk. At first light planes would start taking off and so concentrated were the airfields in Norfolk and Suffolk that a serious safety problem arose as the Flying Fortresses and B-24 Liberators struggled to gain altitude.

With these large planes roaring over the City, life was never to be quite the same for the remaining years of the war. Liberty trucks from these airfields were to arrive nightly at the Cattle Market Park and spill out their young men. And what of these young men? Well their uniforms were smarter than those we were used to seeing, the cloth of finer quality, the men themselves were often sunburnt, and they walked differently – they seemed to roll. They looked at the Norwich girls' drab dresses and were astonished, and the girls were equally surprised at the demonstrative natures of these strange young men whose numbers were to increase so rapidly. They filled the dance-halls; the Lido and the Samson & Hercules overflowed with them. The restaurants and pubs bulged with them as more and more arrived. The ratio of men to girls in the City grew. Girls on the arms of these men were 'chatted up', complimented, and generally attended in a way which, to many, was quite different to their previous experiences with the local boys. And the girls were delighted. With money in their pockets, the generosity of the Americans was at times embarrassing. They brought gifts of stockings and chocolates, tins of food and bunches of flowers. They provided buses to take the girls to camp dances and parties. Understandably not all the locals were delighted with this invasion, especially when they met with indifferent service in restaurants and what they considered unfair competition with the girls. And when our own soldiers arrived home on leave to find their wives or girl-friends otherwise engaged there was the inevitable friction. But any ill-feeling was more than counter-balanced by the many families who asked these Americans to their homes and, in many cases, created lifelong friendships.

During the three years of operations from East Anglian bases, the 8th US Air Force lost over 46,000 men and 6,000 aircraft, and whatever our memories we must feel gratitude.

A unique photograph of American Military Police (Snowdrops) in Bethel Street.

Raid 34

2 August 1942 (Sunday) Alert 02.12 hours

Balloons were raised and hung protectively and anti-aircraft guns opened fire, but despite all this activity enemy planes penetrated the defences and dropped parachute-flares which hung like mobile chandeliers, illuminating the City, as high-explosive bombs and approximately 5,000 incendiaries fell. Some of the latter were of a new type, a combined incendiary and anti-personnel bomb. The unsuspecting householder who ran with a sandbag to smother the flames could have the whole thing explode in his face.

It was assumed in this raid that the incendiaries must have been dropped from aircraft flying at a great height as some remarkable examples of their penetrative power were observed. Asphalt was penetrated to a depth of 5 feet 6 inches and soft ground to a depth of 8 feet 6 inches. Several of the bombs went straight through the concrete roof of Williams' tanning factory in Barrack Street. Another went through an Anderson shelter at 155 Heigham Street, but fortunately for those sheltering there the explosive part of the bomb became detached as it entered the shelter. In several cases when the bomb hit a hard surface the steel nose containing the explosive charge split, loosened the thread, and flew apart from the incendiary section which then burnt out in the normal way. One incendiary fell on the ground between two Anderson shelters at the rear of Bargate Flats in Barrack Street – these were only 18 inches apart and the exploding bomb blew a hole in the bottom corner of one shelter and buckled the side of the other. A 500 kg high explosive bomb fell in the river near the Waterworks and practically demolished the boat-house. Another fell and exploded on Clarke's boot factory in Northumberland Street, which had already been gutted in a previous raid. In Old Palace Road a high-explosive bomb demolished six houses and rendered a large number uninhabitable.

At Napier Street, where the builders had only just finished repairing houses from previous air-raid damage, Mrs Everill, a lady aged 71 who was nearly blind, was with her four daughters and a Mr Allen. They were all sheltering in a brick surface shelter when one section was hit. As the shelter filled with dust they groped their way out to find to their amazement that they were all unhurt.

At the rear of 78 Sprowston Road, a bomb with a slight delay on its fuse penetrated the garden to a great depth, exploded, formed a partial camouflet, and immediately collapsed leaving a large irregular hole with cracks in the ground all round it. The force of the explosion being masked, little damage was occasioned to surrounding property.

At the junction of Branford Road and Spencer Street a 500 kg bomb fell in the centre of the road opposite the Branford Arms public house but failed to explode. The impact of this bomb made a deep hole and was classed as a suspect unexploded bomb resulting in evacuation of the surrounding area. Also in Branford Road a 1,000 kg high-explosive bomb fell on the centre of the roadway and penetrated to some depth before exploding, creating a large crater that extended to houses on both sides of the road.

Only a few people suffered minor injuries in this raid, which was remarkable since a number of shelters had been hit. The basement shelter at 29 Exchange Street was destroyed by fire, the domestic shelter at 52 Napier Street had one compartment destroyed, the communal shelter at 543 Old Palace Road had its brickwork cracked, and the trench shelter in Chapel Field Gardens had an anti-personnel incendiary bomb penetrate the reinforced-concrete roof.

Blackout this week was from 10.31pm to 5.32am which must have been helpful to the Norwich Market stall-holders. The Market carried on as usual throughout the war years. Many of the stalls had to close early to conform with blackout regulations and those that remained open after dark were forced to serve their customers by lights so heavily shaded that only the barest outlines remained visible. Vegetables were never in short supply in Norfolk but many other foodstuffs were and, as the years passed, became very expensive. The stalls lost some of their brilliance – missing were the tall display mounds of oranges, tangerines, lemons, nuts and dates. All imported fruit was in short supply and was either rationed or sold sparingly by the stall-holders.

The stalls were run by women and older men, the young men of the many families that made up the market having been called up for military service. Some of these families had been associated with the Norwich Market for many years and it needed more than a war to break their traditions – so the families of the Minns, the Ponds, the Taylors, the Brands, the Daynes, the Wilsons, and the Manns, to name but a few, carried on.

Raid 35

13 August 1942 (Thursday) Alert 22.41 hours

Some 14 aircraft approached the City and the anti-aircraft guns defending the area went into action. Flares were dropped to the north-west of the City by the one aircraft that succeeded in penetrating the defences. Some 120 incendiaries and three 500 kg high-explosive bombs were dropped by this plane on the north-east boundary of the City. The first of the high-explosive bombs fell on Mousehold Avenue Infants' School where it landed on soft ground some 12 feet from the school wall. The blast caused severe damage to the school and to a number of Council houses opposite.

The second bomb landed on allotments at the rear of 165 Gertrude Road and formed, for some reason, an unusually large crater. The third bomb fell on Mousehold Heath only 50 yards from Playford Road and caused considerable damage to houses there.

The heavy barrage of gunfire seemed to be the reason why this attack was confined to the outskirts of the City.

This week a 250-strong mobile repair gang from London, calling themselves 'the Cockney Sparrows', arrived to help with Norwich's ever-increasing bomb damage. Volunteer building repair teams had in the past months repaired literally thousands of homes and were glad of this extra help.

Adding to the damage caused by bombing were the fragments of shrapnel from our anti-aircraft guns that fell on the City. One of the main reasons for taking cover, these fragments with their razor-like serrated edges were frequently the cause of injury.

August saw the first anniversary of the National Fire Service which was warmly praised for its work during the raids.

In August the Magistrates' Court reverted many public-house licences back to the brewers because of damage sustained in raids. Those named were the Orchard Tavern (Heigham Street), Somerleyton Tavern (Somerleyton Street), Buck (Oak Street), Fountain (St Benedict's Street), Dolphin Inn (Heigham Street), Crown & Angel (St Stephen's Street), Trafford Arms (Grove Road), Anchor (Rising Sun Lane), Jolly Farmers (Farmers Avenue), Swan (King Street), and the Rose (Magdalen Street).

Fines at the Magistrates' Court for failing to have medical examinations after knowingly having been in contact with cases of scabies were much in evidence this month. It was considered that the irritation caused by this disease if not checked could cause loss of sleep and thus be detrimental to the war effort and much effort was made to combat it by the display of posters and appeals by both the Ministry of Health and local doctors.

The medical profession was always ably supported by the mobile units organized by the British Red Cross Society and the Order of St John Joint War Committee. These mobile units were yet again in action, moving at the height of the 'blitz' to help injured civilians, themselves suffering two fatal casualties as a result.

The Samson & Hercules Ballroom at Tombland was a building to which Service personnel flocked at night. An official limit of one thousand people was placed on this hall, but as dancers constantly came and went, often to the Waggon and Horses public house next door, it was difficult to keep a proper count. At first the 'Samson' was a home from home for RAF personnel stationed locally during the Battle of Britain – Douglas Bader, Max Aitken, Stanford Tuck and Johnny Johnson were no strangers there. The bar was often short of beer and spirits but a good trade was done at the coffee and snack bars.

In 1942 the Americans not only took over the RAF airfields, they also took over the Samson & Hercules as well and so for the most part the Norwich

'The local's gone!' The Anchor public house, Rising Sun Lane.

boys were inclined to shun the place, but not so the girls! Many of the latter came to the Samson six nights a week and how they ever carried on their work in factory or office the following day is hard to say. Many friendships made here were cut short when young Americans were reported missing or killed. Sometimes their girlfriends remained at this haunt and occasionally were happily re-united when their boy-friends were picked up in the North Sea or returned to base after having been diverted to other airfields. The ruthlessly efficient white-helmeted American Military Police, known as 'Snowdrops', were always on hand, swiftly removing any misbehaving servicemen from public view. Any fighting was promptly dealt with by the effective use of the nightstick (truncheon) and consequently the Samson had very little trouble of this kind.

A Norwich boy, Gerry Hoey, a prominent figure in the London dance-band world, was brought home by Mr Edward (Teddy) Bush, the well-known Norwich builder and businessman who owned the Samson & Hercules throughout the war years. The Americans loved Gerry Hoey and his Band and when the strains of 'American Patrol' were played they rocked the building, roaring their appreciation, sometimes with tears in their eyes. So the war years went on, and the jitterbugging became wilder.

Mr Bush must be gratefully remembered by the Norwich War Charities. The Samson was only licensed for three dances a week so Mr Bush let the hall, at cost, to various charities for the remaining three nights and this resulted in the raising of many thousands of pounds. Money was sometimes raised by the auctioning of scarce goods, people paying up to £1 for a nip of whisky.

Raid 36 destroyed, among other things, Frazer's Joinery by Whitefriars Bridge. Note the ant-like proportions of the figures in the centre and upper right of the picture.

Raid 36

5 September 1942 (Saturday)
Crash Warning 10.35 hours

Magdalen Street was thronged with early morning shoppers. The Crash Warning was still sounding as a stick of 250 kg high-explosive bombs fell. The enemy aircraft had been flying at a height of 23,000 feet and the only evidence of its presence was a faint vapour trail, hence the short warning. Two bombs fell in the garden of a burnt-out building at the rear on Magdalen Street; had these bombs landed in the street itself casualties would have been heavy. Another bomb fell at the rear of Boots the chemist

of Magdalen Street. This caused very little blast damage; a brick surface shelter only nine feet from the edge of the crater was undamaged.

Frazer's joinery works at St Martin's Palace Plain received a direct hit on the machine-shop which demolished the boiler-house, the debris falling into the river. It was as well there was no fire as these premises were highly flammable but, sadly, four employees were killed and three others injured.

Batson and Webster's boot and shoe factory in Fishergate had a bomb fall in the courtyard where it demolished a cycle-shed, blew a cat into the street, and flung cycles on to the roof. A fire-watchers' brick look-out post in the courtyard was blown over, trapping a number of employees, and here two people were killed and 14 injured.

A fourth bomb fell on Leamon's furniture factory in Calvert Street. The building had previously been gutted by fire and this bomb brought the outside walls crashing to the ground.

In this raid blast damaged a number of houses in Cowgate, Peacock Street, Fishergate, Calvert Street, Pope's Buildings, Cross Lane, St George Street, Colegate and Golden Dog Lane. The shaken shoppers had to pick their way home along streets that were a mosaic of broken glass glittering in the early September sunlight.

This month ARP wardens presented a Silver Challenge Cup to a Scots army unit in gratitude for the help they rendered the City during the recent heavy raids.

The City was also very proud to have collected £410,951 during their ten-week campaign to buy ten Churchill tanks and send them into battle bearing the name 'Norwich'.

Raid 37

19 October 1942 (Monday)
Alert 07.05 hours; Second Alert 10.15 hours

Low cloud curtained the City and the muffled drone of aircraft could be plainly heard. From this cloud dived a Dornier 217 with machine-guns blazing. It flew over the east side of the City in a southerly direction and as it neared the power station released a stick of four 500 kg high-explosive bombs. These fortunately missed the power station and fell on the opposite (south) bank of the river where three exploded. The third, a delayed-action type, failed to penetrate the ground owing to the low level of the attack and was taken away later that day.

At 10.15 the Alert again sounded and this time the enemy plane dived down to a level of 300 feet and swooped across the centre of the City in a northerly direction on an aiming run. After circling it dived again and dropped a stick of four 500 kg bombs. These fell near the heart of the City but did very little damage. One just missed Willow Lane Roman Catholic Infants' School and fell in the Jenny Lind Playground in Pottergate causing a large crater. Nine yards from the lip of this crater a surface shelter stood undamaged, the people inside shaken but unhurt.

Another of the bombs made a direct hit on Edwards & Holmes' shoe factory in Westwick Street. This factory was practically demolished but fortunately the majority of the staff had taken shelter when the crash warning sounded and there were only a few minor casualties.

A bomb fell through the roof of 1 Oak Street, but because of the low level of the attack failed to explode and lay on the floor of a room at ground-level. St Mary's Baptist Chapel in Duke Street, gutted in a previous raid, had its remaining walls destroyed. The Churches of St Margaret and St Swithin and several shops and houses in St Benedict's Street received varying degrees of damage. In Willow Lane, George Borrow House also sustained light damage.

These raids in no way deterred the people of Norwich from queuing for hours to see Clark Gable and Vivien Leigh starring in Gone With The Wind.

The disgust felt by everyone for any person found looting was displayed at the Magistrates' Court today when a man was sentenced to three months hard labour for this offence. Later in the same week another man was given seven years for looting five homes. When you saw people standing by their

The King made a surprise visit to Norwich on Tuesday 13 October 1942, and met service, American and Civil Defence personnel. On his left in this picture is Mrs Ruth Hardy.

The Duke of Kent inspecting members of the Civil Defence on his visit to Norwich.

destroyed homes, bewildered as they tried to save what few things they could from the debris, you could feel little pity for these malefactors.

On Tuesday 13 October 1942 His Majesty King George VI paid a surprise visit to Norwich where, accompanied by Bernard Storey OBE, Town Clerk and ARP Controller, and other Civic dignitaries, he inspected a parade of several hundred men, women and boys representing all branches of the Civil Defence Services. The secret had been so well kept that very few of those on parade knew that they were to be inspected by their King. Several of the Civil Defence workers wore ribbons of medals awarded for distinguished service in recent raids. The youngest in the parade was ARP messenger John Grix to whom the King spoke about the exploits that had won him the BEM. His Majesty was smiling as he said 'I understand you are only fifteen', and young John Grix admitted he had joined the Service below the minimum age. The King also spoke to two other messengers – A J Clover aged 18 of the NFS, and Peter Lomax who was only 16; both these boys had received commendations. Further down the ranks Police Inspector Buttle, recently awarded the BEM for service in connection with bomb reconnaissance, chatted to the King. His Majesty walked on to speak to Mrs Ruth Hardy, who was wearing the uniform of an ARP warden. The King was not familiar with the badge on her shoulder and when told by Mrs Hardy that the letters MAGNA stood for 'Mutual Aid Good Neighbours' Association', he smiled and said 'Mrs Hardy there is too little friendship in the world today. Do keep up this wonderful work when the war is over.'

While in Norwich the King visited the American Servicemen's Club, and here the Lord Mayor was puzzled by a sergeant's proficiency badge but the King knew all about it. The Sergeant, who hailed from San Francisco, ventured to ask His Majesty for his autograph, but the King humorously gestured to the numerous groups of soldiers and intimated that the task would be too great.

Of course, inspections and parades were very much a part of City life during these years. For example, on 26 May 1942 the order of the day was that battle-dress and berets were to be worn, respirators to be carried, and medal ribbons displayed. All 16 branches of the Defence Services were assembled by the Parade Marshal: the Police, National Fire Service, ARP Wardens, messengers, Rescue Parties, First Aid Parties, contingents from First Aid Posts, Mobile Posts, Report Centres, Mortuaries, MAGNA, WVS, British Red Cross, St John's Ambulance, Woodlands Hospital Mobile Canteens, and Rest Centres. On this and like occasions large numbers of citizens would turn out to watch and enjoy the spectacle.

Another photo (as on page 14) from the Luftwaffe booklet of Norwich targets.

Raid 38

3 November 1942 (Tuesday) Alert 07.45 hours

A Dornier 217, diving below low-lying cloud, swept across the City at roof top level and dropped four 500 kg high-explosive bombs. One fell through the roof of Surrey Street Bus Station. Coming down at an angle it penetrated the top of a single-decker bus and crashed through to the ground where it failed to explode. If it had exploded numerous casualties would have resulted as the Bus Station was crowded at the time. The other three bombs fell in the kitchen garden of 53 All Saints' Green where, failing to explode, they lay on the surface like three large marrows. This aircraft also machine-gunned several streets in the vicinity of College Road, Earlham Road and Lincoln Street and although there was some damage to roofs nobody was hurt.

There was an appeal this week from the Chief Billeting Officer for householders to set aside one or two rooms for those rendered homeless. He also urged everybody to make mutual arrangements for alternative accommodation with

GB **9**, BB 19. Nr. 24: Omnibusgroßgarage in Norwich (Norfolkshire). Großgarage und Omnibus-Station der "Eastern Counties Omnibus Co. Ltd"; für 170 Wagen; Tanklager für 22 700 l Brennstoff. 1,6 ha Fläche.

friends or relations, preferably in another district, in the event of their homes being destroyed or badly damaged.

A Census of Laid-Up Vehicles was being carried out. Ninety per cent of the world's rubber supply was now in enemy hands and the Government needed to know where all unused tyres were to be found.

The motorist's life was not a happy one. This month many trades people were fined for the misuse of petrol when police inspected the car park at the Sprowston Road dog racing track.

With the year rapidly drawing to a close one strange fact was noted: comparing the health of citizens during the year 1942 with that prevailing in the pre-war years the medical authorities were astounded at the high standard which was being maintained. Considering the disruption of normal ways of living – the lack of certain foods and fruit with the consequent change in customary diet; the long hours of working plus the time spent in Civil Defence duties; the curtailment of means of transportation – the health of the City remained remarkably good. The outbreaks of minor epidemics among schoolchildren were not serious, and the general health of citizens was excellent.

During the early part of June 1942 many homes in Norwich were relieved by news of husbands or sons held prisoner by the Japanese. For many months after the fall of Hong Kong, Singapore and Burma a dread silence of suspense had hung over Norwich and the County of Norfolk. This had now been partly broken and a ray of hope for the New Year pierced the dark despair.

Raid 39

5 December 1942 (Saturday) Alert 12.43 hours

Anti-aircraft guns roared into action as a Dornier 217 approached the City. The pilot of the plane must have been somewhat shaken by this activity, as he narrowly missed the cable of a barrage balloon at Thorpe. When machine-guns added their weight to the defensive fire he jettisoned his bombs, a stick of four 500 kg high explosives, which fell 150 yards south of a gun site straddling Heartsease Lane. These bombs all proved to be of the delayed-action type and on Tuesday 8th they were removed by the Bomb Disposal Squad.

At a large house next to the Congregational Church in Chapel Field East the Boys' Messenger Service had their Headquarters. The stables at the back of the house next to the Theatre Royal were used as a repair shop for their bicycles and motor-cycles. One section of the Messengers was attached to each of the four Wardens' Divisions, while another was attached to the Report Centre. Each section was divided into four units, each with its own area of responsibility and under the charge of a unit leader drawn from the ranks.

These boisterous youngsters, who happily rode through the height of the blitz, were not so brave about the ghost stories that surrounded this house. They were always wary of strange noises and of being left in a room alone. These stories must have been enlarged and elaborated on by the older members of the unit. Many tales were told of their exploits and not least of them, in size anyhow, was the tale of how one of their leaders went into the stables only to be confronted by two elephants. On rushing back into the house and inquiring in no uncertain manner what the devil was going on, Peter Gooch, one of the boys, confessed that he had been talking to a member of the circus group that were appearing at the Theatre Royal that week and had offered him the use of the stables for the elephants in return for free tickets to the show. Although the unit was usually referred to as 'the Boys' Messenger Service', they did in fact include girls in their number. Names that can be remembered were George Crow, Morris Cracknell, K Yaxley, Henry Hunsell, Peter Gooch, Rose Mathews, Brian Cooper, K Turner, Stanley Taylor and, of coarse, John Grix and Peter Lomax both of whom received the BEM.

During the year 1942, 106 Alerts had been sounded covering a total of 99 hours. It had been a bad year for Norwich with a large number of buildings destroyed and many more damaged in the raids.

Raid 40

1 January 1943 (Friday) Alert 13.35 hours

With clouds at 800 feet and heavy rain falling, a Dornier 217 swooped across the City from a south-westerly direction. It turned and following a north-easterly course dropped a stick of eight 50 kg high-explosive bombs.

Seven fell to the south of the City Station Goods Yard and the other to the north side. The enemy bomber then opened up with machine-guns and damaged the roofs of a number of houses in the Spencer Street and Beaconsfield Road area, and after dropping two 500 kg high-explosive bombs on Mousehold Heath it made off. All these bombs detonated and, with the damage caused by the machine-gunning, 429 houses were battered and six people received minor injuries.

The first bomb exploded in a small garden at the rear of 18 Haslip's Opening, demolishing a large shed and damaging the rears of numbers 17, 18 and 19. The body of a man was found in number 19 but it was later proved that he had been dead for several days. The second fell in the garden at the rear of 24 Russell Street, damaging numbers 20, 22 and 24. Bomb number three fell in Russell Street hitting the wall of St Barnabas's Church near the roof, where it exploded. The Parish Hall opposite was damaged by blast. The fourth bomb landed in the gardens at the rear of 52 Derby Street and damaged adjacent properties with blast. Bomb number five scored a direct hit on 60 Derby Street and this house, together with numbers 58 and 62, was completely destroyed.

The sixth bomb fell on the pavement in front of the Derby Arms public house making a small crater. It damaged gas-mains and severely damaged the public house. Bomb number seven exploded, amid the rubble of premises already damaged in previous raids, at the corner of Derby Street and Heigham Street. A domestic brick shelter was within three yards of the crater but suffered no structural damage. The blast from this bomb severely damaged the north side of the already stricken Derby Arms public house. The last of this stick of 50 kg high explosives demolished the premises of the Croft Joinery Company in Chatham Street.

The first of the two 500 kg high explosive bombs fell on Mousehold Heath near Gilman Road, at the rear of 214 Gertrude Road. It detonated and made a crater 28 feet across. The blast caused rather extensive damage to 12 houses. The second 500 kg bomb also fell on Mousehold Heath, about 20 yards south of the Pavilion and left a medium-sized crater.

All this must have been a most unwelcome herald on New Year's Day.

A New Year's message from the Sheriff appeared in the Eastern Evening News. Although one of hope at the time it now seems ironic. It read: 'I would specially urge that we all shall demand and prepare for the rebuilding of Norwich in the early post-war period on lines that will command the respect and thanks of coming generations and that youth shall demand of politicians that

the Councils of the World shall take such steps as will eliminate the possibility of war in the future.'

Supplies of utility furniture reached the City's shops this month. This was to be supplied only to those people who were setting up home for the first time, providing they had married before the beginning of 1941, or were expecting a baby.

The Government were worried as to why people were no longer having so many children. A heavy drop in the birth-rate over the past year had been noted and a 'baby bonus' was being suggested.

However busy people were in these war days it seemed that some were not busy enough. At the Magistrates' Court this month a man, engaged on essential war work, was fined for being late for work on 24 mornings out of 37 – it cost him £5!

Raid 41

18 March 1943 (Monday) Alert 22.30 hours.

Enemy aircraft attacked several times during the period of this Alert and on each occasion our anti-aircraft guns came into action. The planes that penetrated this barrage dropped 60 SBCSO incendiaries (a spring-band type containing a cluster of small incendiary units and a 12lb explosive charge) and number of phosphorus bombs. Considering the number of these bombs that were dropped the damage caused was remarkably slight. There was, however, one major fire and this occurred at Harmer's clothing factory in St Andrews Street. This firm, founded in 1825, had been attacked in previous raids. It was engaged on Government contracts for the supply of uniforms to the Armed Forces and Civil Defence, just as it had been during the First World War. In 1915 its production had been two tons of uniforms daily. The resilience of this factory was quite remarkable. Each time part of the works was destroyed alternative space was rented and, at one point during the war, the business was carried on at seven different addresses. In this raid most of the original factory was gutted by fire.

Everyone was depressed this week. A warning had been given that clothing coupons might only be 48 per head in the next issue. The present book contained 60 coupons. A decision would not be taken until nearer the time of the next issue and in the meantime labour, materials, and the shipping position would be assessed. But it was still felt that there would be a reduction and the following list will give some idea what this would mean.

Clothing coupons

Ration Period to 31 May 1942

Cloth – coupons needed per yard depends on the width, for example, a yard of cloth woollen 36 inches wide requires three coupons and cotton or other cloth two coupons. Knitting wool, one coupon is needed for two ounces.

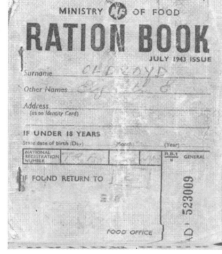

MEN AND BOYS	Adults	Children
Unlined mackintosh or cape	9	7
Other mackintoshes, raincoat, overcoat	16	11
Coat, jacket, blazer and like garments	13	8
Waistcoat, pullover, cardigan, jersey	5	3
Trousers (other than fustian or corduroy)	8	6
Fustian or corduroy trousers	5	5
Shorts	5	3
Overalls, dungarees and like garments	6	4
Dressing-gown, bathing-gown or pair pyjamas	8	6
Shirt, combinations – woollen	8	6
Pants, vest, bathing-costume, child's blouse	4	2
Shirt, combinations – other material	5	4
Pair socks, or stockings	3	1
Collar, tie or two handkerchiefs	1	1
Scarf, pair of gloves or mittens	2	2
Pair of slipper or galoshes	4	2
Pair of boots or shoes	7	3
Pair of leggings, gaiters or spats	3	2

WOMEN AND GIRLS		
Coat, raincoat, lined mackintosh	14	11
Jacket, short coat	11	8
Dress, gown, frock – woollen	11	8
Dress, gown, frock – other material	7	5
Gym tunic, girl's skirt with bodice	8	6
Blouse, sports shirt, cardigan, jumper	5	3
Skirt, divided skirt	7	5
Overalls, dungarees, and like garments	6	4
Apron, pinafore	3	2
Pyjamas	8	6
Nightdress	6	5
Petticoat, slip, combinations, cami-knickers	4	3
Other undergarments, including corsets	3	2
Pair of stockings	2	1
Pair of socks, collar, tie, or two handkerchiefs	1	1
Scarf, pair of gloves or mittens, muff	2	2
Pair of slippers, boots or shoes	5	3

A precious ration booklet for 1943–44.

Raid 42

5 May 1943 (Wednesday) Alert 02.34 hours

A large number of our own aircraft were returning from operations when several enemy planes followed them in over the coast and approached the City. Because of the proximity of friendly aircraft our anti-aircraft defences had to remain silent. The north-west perimeter of the City was suddenly lit by flares and shortly afterwards phosphorus and explosive incendiary bombs rained down.

In St Andrew Street Bagshaws', the scrap-metal merchants, had a small fire on their premises and in Exchange Street a crater six feet across damaged water-mains. Opposite 41 Bridewell Alley a bomb fell on the path between St Andrew's Church and Matthes' bakery shop. Matthes was severely damaged and blazing debris, blown to the Church, caused several small fires which were quickly extinguished. In Queen Street St Michael-at-Plea Church had an unexploded incendiary, which was later removed. The Cathedral Tea Rooms were gutted by fire and the adjoining premises badly damaged. In Hellesdon Mill Lane, near Wallace King's furniture repository, a bomb exploded against a four-ton lorry and

Post G7. Lubbock Close, Elizabeth Fry Road.

destroyed it. In Hellesdon Hall Road fields around Gowing's farm had six exploded incendiaries but little damage was caused. An unexploded phosphorus bomb landed in the back garden of number 22 Larkman Lane and this type of bomb also landed in the back gardens of 30 Larkman Lane and 3 and 8 Beecheno Road. Number 584 Dereham Road had an unexploded phosphorus bomb on the grass verge outside and phosphorus was splashed over the wooden fence. In a straight line from a point west of the junction of Marl Pit Lane and Dereham Road to Hellesdon four more bombs fell on open ground but caused no damage. A number of these bombs fell on the Larkman Lane Estate but remarkably few of them struck property. Of the few that did 6 and 29 Cadge Close had fires in their bedrooms and 4, 14, 15 and 30 Earlham Green Lane also had bedroom fires. At 30 Earlham Green Lane and 71 Cadge Road incendiaries fell on a staircase and 129 Cadge Road and 469 Dereham Road had bedroom fires. All the bombs on this estate exploded but happily all were extinguished by wardens and fireguards. A further nine phosphorus and nine incendiary bombs fell on Bunkers Hill Wood in Larkman Lane and exploded.

In May the City's rivers must have looked inviting on sunny afternoons and the rowing-boats for hire on the 'back' river did a brisk trade. No pleasure-craft were permitted on the Broads or waterways and trips to the coast were forbidden, so people drifted peacefully along in the back-waters of Norwich and for a while forgot the war. Around the parks and gardens very few districts had escaped the attention of workmen busily engaged in removing the iron railings for scrap. Their removal was, in some cases, not regretted as these railings were often criticized for their general ugliness and those with spiked tops were considered positively dangerous. The only difficulty experienced was in trying to find a substitute, as all materials were in short supply.

In June an unfortunate incident was recorded. At 8.10am on Wednesday 23 June 1943, the pilot of an American Typhoon fighter accidentally discharged his machine-guns while flying towards the west of the City. A number of houses were struck by bullets and damage occurred in those streets lying between Dereham Road and Earlham Road. Fortunately no casualties were reported and this must have proved a great relief to the young pilot.

The NAAFI in Norwich in the later years of the war was quite a place. Buntings' old building in Rampant Horse Street (now Marks & Spencer) which had been gutted by fire in the 1942 blitz, had been rebuilt to house this branch of the NAAFI which was considered to be one of the finest in the country.

Mrs Laura Johnson who worked there during the war years remembers the large foyer, with its glass kiosk for the sale of cigarettes, around which were dotted comfortable armchairs. Behind the kiosk the old ironwork lift, which had miraculously escaped damage in the fire, would take you up to the second floor and here a carpeted lounge and dance-floor were situated. The third floor housed the canteen while down in the basement a bar and facilities for billiards and table-tennis were available.

The building also boasted a sewing-room, writing-room, and a number of bathrooms. The whole atmosphere was of a standard of luxury not generally found by members of the British Forces.

In front of this building Curl's old site had been cleared and on its foundations a huge static water tank had been built. This tank held 270,000 gallons of water and was one of the largest in the country. The Civil Defence were determined not to be short of water in the event of further bombing. This water-tank was occasionally used as a swimming pool, when a member of the Forces had had more than a usually good night. These antics were frowned on by the police who pursued the culprits round the tank to the delight of the watching crowd.

◀ *Advertisement for a morale-boosting Carnival, in aid of war charities.*

KEEP A DATE!

IT IS

Saturday, 7th August

Come for a Spree to

Recreation Sports Ground

RECREATION ROAD, EARLHAM ROAD

From 2.30 until 9 p.m.

Grand Carnival

Tickets on Sale from the Wardens, M.A.G.N.A., Home Guards, Special Constables, Scouts, Cubs, Fire Watchers, N.F.S., R.O.C., W.V.S., in fact all the troops on our side

Adults, 5d., Children under 14, 3d.

Any Prizes, Contributions, etc., gratefully received at

DIV. I HEADQUARTERS, CIVIL DEFENCE, WEST PARADE, EARLHAM ROAD, NORWICH

ORGANISED BY WARDENS OF GROUP "G"

IN AID OF THE LOCAL WAR CHARITIES

ROBERTS PRINTERS (NORWICH) LTD., TEN BELL LANE, NORWICH.

◀◀ *Curl's basement became a water reservoir as Messrs Bond's reopened in Orford Place.*

Raid 43

7 October 1943 (Thursday) Alert 20.38 hours

The Observer Corps reported that more than 150 hostile aircraft had crossed the coast, the majority of them heading for London. About 25 enemy aircraft remained over Norfolk and made scattered attacks on airfields in the county. 24 barrage balloons were raised over the City and anti-aircraft guns opened fire driving off the two enemy planes approaching the City from the south-west. At the same time a third aircraft appeared and, on encountering the flak, circled to the east and dropped four 500 kg high-explosive bombs on the extreme boundary of the area covered by Wardens' Post L73 which was situated at Long John Hill near Barrett Road. Three of the bombs fell on to marshland causing slight damage to a river-bank at Old Lakenham. The fourth exploded near railway lines creating a crater approximately 30 feet in diameter which extended halfway across the double lines of track blocking both of them.

At this period the Medical Officer of Health was worried by the reduction in the City's population which had dropped to 106,100 – the harassing times provided little inducement for people to have families.

*Post G8.
Colman Road.*

An appeal was made for both domestic and industrial coal-users to at least equal last year's economies. The mines were short of manpower and it was felt necessary to institute a compulsory call-up similar to that for the Armed Forces, although volunteers were still encouraged. A minimum of 720,000 miners had to be maintained.

One good thing this week – the joyous sound of the bells of the Church of St John de Sepulchre in Ber Street were heard for the first time since before 1940. Recently repaired, the authorities saw no reason why the bells should not be tested as the invasion, which they were to have heralded, was now no longer a threat.

Raid 44

6 November 1943 (Saturday) Alert 22.50 hours

One enemy plane dived across the City and dropped phosphorus bombs. Four minutes later a second aircraft dropped several high-explosive bombs. The latter all had impact fuses and landed on fields of kale east of the Municipal Golf Course in Bluebell Road. Flares were then dropped to the west of the City and our anti-aircraft batteries opened fire, only to cease firing after two salvoes – the reason for this was not recorded.

At Beaumont Place an empty container landed. It was the type that carried 500 ABB incendiaries and as this was a new type the Report Centre was hurriedly advised.

Small fires broke out in Onley Street, Lincoln Street, Portland Street, College Road, Glebe Road, Grange Road, Spelman Road, Henley Road, Mornington Road and Unthank Road.

Nobody seems to have been hurt during this raid but only those who have experienced a fire in their homes can understand all it entails. Even a small fire leaves in its wake saturated carpets and furniture, blackened wallpaper, smoke-stained ceilings and the smell of wet burnt material that remains detectable to the nostrils for weeks after the scars of the fire have been removed.

On the night of the 14 November a violent storm broke out over Norwich and 15 barrage balloons were struck by lightning. They burst into flames and slowly drifted to earth. What with the noise of the thunder and the sight of these burning balloons many people thought that an air raid was in progress.

During this month a 19 year old girl was fined on two charges of being absent from work without reasonable excuse; it cost her 10s. At the same Magistrates' Court a man was fined £25 for supplying two and a half gallons of petrol without coupons.

Many of the sad cases heard at the Juvenile Court were very much a product of the times. Two children were brought before the Court charged with begging from American Air Force men. Child begging was not yet a widespread nuisance but it was one which appeared to be increasing. A year previously to find a youngster begging on the streets of Norwich was virtually unheard of. Its recrudescence, said the Magistrate, was due to the fact that a handful of youngsters found the uniformed newcomers from the other side of the Atlantic almost always kindly disposed towards children. They had made the initial mistake of tipping too frequently and too lavishly and the news of these monetary gifts was passed on to other children.

The American Servicemen in our midst often tried too hard to please and this was invariably misunderstood by the proud and independent Norfolk people. Although there were similarities in language our ways of life were very different and we had to adjust. Parents winced at the American slang and the 'jitterbugging' antics of their teenage daughters. The Americans also had to adjust. They had to learn to drink our warm beer and to move about the narrow winding streets of Norwich in the stygian blackout.

Coming as they did from a country where there was either no blackout, or at most a dim-out, this could not have been easy.

In their off-duty periods American Servicemen found the English bicycle, with its three-speed gear, a great source of convenience and amusement. On their airfields where diners (mess-halls) could be miles from their areas of work the bicycle was very useful. The amusement they obtained in their leisure hours from these, to them, strange machines was immense. They often painted them in an array of colours with stripes and spots for easy identification.

The Americans found their way to 'Dodger's' bicycle shop in Chapel Street and here they purchased, or hired at 1s an hour, a variety of machines and delighted in the odd array of penny-farthings, bone-shakers and mobile bedsteads the Dodger family had in their collection. Chapel Street rang to the laughter of their girlfriends as these automobile-minded men from large cities tried to ride bicycles for the first time after attempting to put trouser-clips round their calves, and local residents stood amazed to see young American officers laughing and joining in the antics of the enlisted men.

This month the Americans staged indoor baseball at Blackfriars Hall. League games were being played in different camps in Norfolk and north Suffolk and the semi-finals were to be held in Norwich. 150 pumpkins were sent from Houghton Hall for American Thanksgiving Day and the Yanks, in turn, invited Norwich people to their Thanksgiving parties at which prominent stars of stage, screen and radio were often present.

At about this time Norwich witnessed a rather unusual wedding, believed to be the first of its kind to take place in England. On 4 December an American servicewoman was married to an Englishman. During their three years of operations from East Anglian bases something like 50,000 American servicemen had been married to British girls but here was something different.

The number of alerts during 1943 was 95 with a total duration of 54 hours. The Crash Warning was sounded 50 times with a total duration of 19 hours 8 and a half minutes.

The air raid on the night of 6 November 1943 is recorded by the Wardens' Service as being the last time that the shriek of falling bombs was heard in the blacked-out streets of Norwich; the last time that our citizens were to stand by their burnt and damaged homes. From then on enemy air activity was to be confined to occasional reconnaissance flights, and we could now work out the cost of it all.

American servicemen try out a weird selection of cycles from Dodger's shop.

After the Raids

Norwich Air Raids 1940–1943

Casualties

	Killed	Injured
1940	60	190
1941	21	104
1942	258	784
1943	1	14
TOTAL	**340**	**1,092**

The year 1944 saw very little activity by enemy aircraft over the region but a vast increase of movement by our own air force which brought a new form of danger to the City. On returning from operations over enemy-held territory these planes often came back damaged with shrapnel holes clearly visible in wings, tail-planes and fuselage.

Damage to Dwelling-houses

Destroyed	2,082
Seriously damaged	2,651
Moderately damaged (including those slightly damaged)	25,621
TOTAL	**30,354**

'Bag-O-Bolts' returns her wounded with one engine ablaze and 400 flak and bullet holes.

On the night of 22 April 1944 American Liberator bombers were returning from daylight operations. The crews had not been trained in night flying so some confusion in landing these aircraft was inevitable. To make matters worse enemy night-fighters had infiltrated this force. The Liberators, with their navigation lights on, were sitting targets for the enemy fighters as they circled the landing-fields.

After this engagement it was thought that some 14 American bombers were shot down in various parts of the county, one crashing on outskirts of the City at the Tuckswood.

In 1944 American aircraft flew many missions from the two airfields near Norwich. The 467th Bomb Group from Rackheath, known to their buddies as the 'Rackheath Aggies', flew a total of 212 missions and their total sorties were 5,538. This group set up an American record for bombing accuracy. Their aircraft bore such names as Jack the Ripper, Blond

Bomber, Belle of the East, Wolves Inc., Perils of Pauline, and Bugs Bunny. The celebrated Witchcraft flew 130 missions without an abort, and seemed to be always in the sky. Nearer to the City the 458th Bomb Groups stationed at Horsham St Faiths flew 240 missions with a total of 5,759 sorties. It was in November 1944 that a young American pilot of the 458th Bomb Group fought desperately with the controls of his crippled B-24 bomber as he plunged towards the densely populated area of Heigham Street. After hitting the tower of St Philip's Church he finally managed to crash the bomber on open ground just off Barker Street. All nine of the crew were killed but his skill and courage prevented the loss of many civilian lives.

In the early hours of 6 June large formations of Liberators, Dakotas and gliders were seen passing overhead and the whole sky vibrated with activity. The hopes of months had now become reality – D-day had arrived.

On 26 June a strange noise was chard as a new silhouette crossed over the City, a small toy-like plane with a tail of fire. We were later to learn that this was Hitler's secret weapon, the V1. At night the V1s could be plainly seen, the long tail of exhaust gases glowing in the sky. A considerable number of these flying-bombs passed over the area but none exploded within the City boundaries.

At 6.10pm on 26 September a very loud explosion was heard which seemed to come from the direction of Ranworth but no information could be obtained as to its origin. Then at 10.55am the next day another explosion occurred north of the City and later on two more were heard, one from the general direction of Great Yarmouth and the other from the Bramerton area. At no time was any sign of a missile seen or heard. On 29 September there was an explosion at Coltishall followed by one at Whitlingham.

Part of an official summary of the warnings throughout the war.

On 3 October 1944 at 7.45pm the whole City was shaken by a large detonation and superficial blast damage to property in the Mile Cross and Dereham Road areas was reported. On the north side of Hellesdon Golf Course debris from a missile was strewn over an area of some 600 yards and a shallow crater 4 feet deep and 32 by 27 feet wide supplemented the bunkers on the course.

An ARP report referred to this missile as 'Big Ben', their code word for the V2 rocket, which indeed it was. This terrible weapon that rained down on London that year was falling around our City but again fate decreed that none should fall within its boundaries.

In 1944 the Alert sounded 76 times covering a total time of 42 hours 22 minutes.

In July 1944, in accordance with Government plans, it was decided to evacuate 2,500 women and children from London to Norwich because of the danger of flying-bombs. The Chief Billeting Officer's Department, with the assistance of 20 full-time wardens, set about the job of canvassing for accommodation.

On 16 July the first batch of some 400 evacuees arrived in Norwich and were temporarily housed in the Crome and Stuart School. Corporation rent-collectors had obtained offers of accommodation on the Plumstead Estate and the majority of these evacuees were housed in that area, with the exception of several large families who naturally wished to stay together and just would not fit into these modest houses. It was arranged, therefore, for the larger type homes on the south side of the City to be canvassed for voluntary billets. On one long road of large houses just one householder volunteered to take a child, a number of other householders complained bitterly of the shortage of servants and kindly offered accommodation to clean girls of 16 to 17 years of age who were willing to help in the house. The Billeting Officer found that many houses in this area had a tendency to shrink. Some large houses called upon, according to

A direct hit on the shelter in Raynham Street. Fourteen people lost their lives.

the householders, had only three bedrooms. In other cases the number of residents in a house increased amazingly, house-holders claimed they had five, six and sometimes seven persons living with them while their neighbours knew of only two and wondered where the rest were hiding. Because of this, official advice was sought and records at the City Hall consulted. In one case a worthy citizen had glibly stated that he had only three bedrooms and three downstairs rooms when in fact he had seven bedrooms and four ground-floor rooms, excluding kitchen and pantry. All houses in The Close were canvassed, with negative results.

On 3 August 1944 a further 370 evacuees arrived including 60 unaccompanied children, and they were welcomed at the George White School Rest Centre. Unaccompanied children and mothers with one or two children were billeted in the City's smaller houses, but again there was the problem of finding accommodation for large families to avoid splitting them up. When a further 360 evacuees, including 36 unaccompanied children, arrived at Angel Road Rest Centre the same difficulty remained and by 10 August some 90 evacuees still remained unbilleted and were transferred to the Dowson School Rest Centre. A special meeting of the Emergency Committee was called on 11 August 1944 to discuss the problem. At this meeting compulsory billeting was not looked on favourably by the Chief Billeting Officer and it was suggested that if essential furniture could be found many families could be housed in requisitioned property and Nissen huts. Several families had already been put into Nissen huts and attention was drawn to the conditions that many of them were living in. One of these huts had been used to accommodate three adults and six children and all that had been provided for them were six bunks, blankets, one small table and four folding garden chairs, one kettle, a frying-pan and two saucepans, all cooking being done over a small coal stove. Water had to be obtained from adjacent houses. These huts were constructed of corrugated iron, the heat was unbearable in hot weather and they were very cold at night when the damp caused condensation.

It was decided to leave the question of compulsory billeting until the next batch of evacuees arrived on 13 August. There were 349 of them, including 36 unaccompanied children and these were received at the Lakenham Rest Centre. Yet again the small families and the unaccompanied children were quickly found quarters but over 100 remained unhoused, most of them being mothers with three or more children. These unfortunates were transferred to the Dowson School Rest Centre to join the earlier arrivals from the Angel Road School Rest Centre. A further 360

evacuees arrived on 31 August and were received at the Norman School Rest Centre. These were, in the main, smaller families and 310 were easily billeted, again in the 'small houses', on the same day. The remaining 50 stayed at the Rest Centre overnight and were billeted in requisitioned houses the following day.

On 8 September 1944 the Government announced that all evacuations were cancelled, but on this date a further 270 evacuees turned up at Thorpe Station and were accommodated at the Colman Road School Rest Centre. By 6.30pm 200 of them had been found billets 'in the smaller houses' and the remainder were put into requisitioned houses the following day.

In a report, 'Billeting 1944', one warden is recorded as saying 'What damned hypocrites' after interviewing ladies who told him obvious lies regarding the size of their houses and the number of people living in them, as they were seen hurrying off to church carrying prayer-books.

Billeting 1944

Summary of the Billeting of Evacuees in Norwich

Type of house	Number of evacuees billeted	
	Adults	**Children**
Council houses	428	715
Cottages	145	183
Terraced houses (working class)	574	833
Medium-sized houses	109	140
Large residential houses	37	43
Totals	**1,293**	**1,914**

Grand Total 3,207

To this number must be added 350 evacuees who were billeted in empty requisitioned houses and Nissen huts.

VE Day in Norwich Market Place.

VE Day

On 8 May 1945 war in Europe ended. It was a dull cloudy morning in Norwich as early buses carried workers who were in some doubt as to the time the Victory in Europe Holiday Celebrations were to begin, so they went to work to find out.

At 9am at Britannia Barracks 1000 servicemen attended a drumhead service and were then given the rest of the day off to join in the general celebrations. At this point nobody seemed to know what form these celebrations were to take. With children in mind many street parties were being arranged. In Victoria Street a Victory tea party was being prepared by Inspector Adams of the NSPCC, his wife and Mrs Leech.

Trestle-tables were erected in front of a bombed site on which the children were busily building a large bonfire surmounted by an effigy of Hitler.

It rained slightly but then the sun shone as more and more people arrived in the City from the surrounding country areas although some, for the first time in many years, visited the seaside.

During the morning a Civic Service was held at St Peter Mancroft Church and large crowds watched the procession of Civic dignitaries who walked from the City Hall to the church. The City Hall was dressed with streamers and on its roof the flags of the Allied Nations fluttered as church bells began to peal their Victory message.

In the ruins of St Mary's Baptist Chapel in St Mary's Plain, which had been destroyed in the raids of 1942, the rubble was swept away, a few seats put out and a Thanksgiving Service was held. It was estimated that between 300 and 400 people stood amid the ruins of the church as Dr Gilbert Laws conducted the service.

The crowds in the City became dense but there was still little to do and after five and a half years of war they were all quietly sober as they gravitated towards The Walk and the Market Place. British Servicemen began pouring into the City and during the course of the day 2,000 of them visited the YMCA, where 200 of them were provided with a free lunch. In the evening they were entertained by a concert which included the White Aces and the Ray Springfield Band. As the buses became full cars and vans accumulated passengers on their roofs and running-boards and the crowds became such that progress through the streets was very slow.

It was mid-afternoon and still the restraint held, but the fuse was lit when a group of soldiers, unable to stand the calm any longer, grabbed a group of girls, linked arms, and began to sing.

The stress of those long years of war exploded. The traditional East Anglian reserve broke. Everyone turned to whoever was nearest and started chatting animatedly. The amazing sight of British and American airmen walking arm in arm was cheered.

As darkness fell Norwich became a blaze of light with all the Civic buildings floodlit. The exclamations of joy from young children born of the blackout was to bring tears to the eyes of many who watched them. Fireworks and Vercy lights reflected the faces of the excited crowds as they danced and shouted.

American Liberators and RAF Mosquitoes, dropping scores of coloured flares, flew overhead with all their lights on, and were caught in the searchlights which continually swept the City skies. Other searchlights picked out, in turn, all the prominent buildings and the 'V' sign was flashed intermittently into the sky until the small hours. By midnight the crowds were ecstatic with happiness. The City's tall lamp-posts offered the only vantage-points left and servicemen climbed them. One American soldier's enthusiasm was such that he lost his balance and hurtled down into the crowd. As he struck the pavement the crowd buzzed with rumours of his death but it was later learned that his only injury was a broken wrist.

A young policeman standing on duty at Jarrolds' corner was grabbed by a young girl who entwined him in her arms as she rained kisses on his face while her companions danced round them. The officer looked somewhat embarrassed at first and then good-heartedly resigned himself to the onslaught, as did his colleagues, and the crowd loved them for it. Somebody started singing the 'Conga' and people quickly grabbed each other's waists in this snake-like dance, which started somewhere on The

Walk and grew until it moved up Guildhall Hill and back again.

By now the main idea seemed to be to embrace whoever was nearest, not just the odd policeman. Norwich streets could never have witnessed such scenes before. For its citizens the war was over, their men folk might still be called upon to fight in the Far East against the Japanese, but the bombing was ended. The skyline, reflected in the searchlights, was not too badly scarred. The beams crossing the sky picked out the City Hall, the Cathedral, the Castle, the Guildhall and many churches – there was much for Norwich to celebrate that night.

If on a sunny afternoon in 2002 and the years to follow you walk up on to Mousehold Hill and look down on the 'Fine City' spread before you, be thankful – 'corse Bor we dam' near lorst the lot'.

In the author's collection of photographs of Norwich at War is this picture. Neither the unit shown nor any of the people in the picture can be identified. Can you help? If you are able to assist, please e-mail norwichatwar@poppyland.co.uk with your information, or write to the publishers. Any information supplied will be put up on the resource web site associated with the book at www.poppyland.co.uk/resources.

Appendices

Appendix 1

Norwich Civil Defence Organisation

The many branches of the Civil Defence services had to be ready for any emergency: the Wardens to report any incident and render initial essential assistance; Rescue Parties to deal with trapped casualties in dangerously insecure or demolished buildings; ambulanecs to transport casualties; gas specialists to deal speedily with any emergency caused by a gas attack; and even the Mortuary Service had inevitably to be prepared.

Two-way communication was essential to facilitate the prompt reporting of each incident, thus enabling the Control Centre to issue the necessary orders for dispatching whatever equipment or personnel were required. At the time of these raids each Wardens' Post was connected by telephone to the Control Centre which, in turn, had direct lines to each of the Rescue Party depots, the Ambulance depots, and the First Aid Posts. In the event of a telephone breakdown the help of the Home Guard and Messenger Boy service had been organized to supplement the Special Communications service of the Police Force and National Fire Service. These last two services, although independent of Civil Defence administration, acted in close liaison at all times. The Control Centre itself started operations beneath the War Memorial in front of the City Hall, a building previously used for the storage of market stalls. At a later date it was transferred to a building in Heigham Grove until finally suitable premises

City & County Borough of Norwich Civil Defence Wardens' Service and Fireguard Organisation

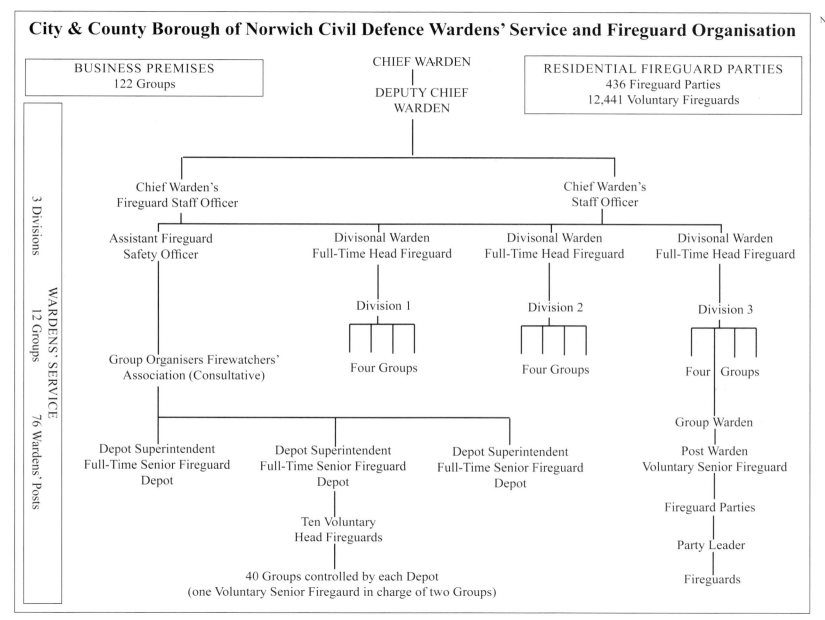

BUSINESS PREMISES
122 Groups

CHIEF WARDEN

DEPUTY CHIEF WARDEN

RESIDENTIAL FIREGUARD PARTIES
436 Fireguard Parties
12,441 Voluntary Fireguards

3 Divisions

WARDENS' SERVICE

12 Groups

76 Wardens' Posts

Chief Warden's
Fireguard Staff Officer

Chief Warden's
Staff Officer

Assistant Fireguard
Safety Officer

Divisonal Warden
Full-Time Head Fireguard

Divisonal Warden
Full-Time Head Fireguard

Divisonal Warden
Full-Time Head Fireguard

Division 1

Division 2

Division 3

Group Organisers Firewatchers'
Association (Consultative)

Four Groups

Four Groups

Four Groups

Depot Superintendent
Full-Time Senior Fireguard
Depot

Depot Superintendent
Full-Time Senior Fireguard
Depot

Depot Superintendent
Full-Time Senior Fireguard
Depot

Group Warden

Post Warden
Voluntary Senior Fireguard

Ten Voluntary
Head Fireguards

Fireguard Parties

Party Leader

40 Groups controlled by each Depot
(one Voluntary Senior Fireguard in charge of two Groups)

Fireguards

were specially constructed on Ipswich Road.

In the Control Centre 24 telephone lines dealt with all incoming and outgoing calls. Messengers on foot took incoming reports to the Controller, the City Engineer, and the Medical Officer of Health or one of his deputies. Also present in the Control Centre with the ARP Officer were a Rest Centre Officer and a representative of the Wardens' service, together with representatives from each of the Post Office Telephone, Electricity, Gas, and Waterworks undertakings. A Gas Identification Officer, if necessary, was at hand, with liaison officers from the Police Force and the Fire Service. The City Architect plotted the incidents on a large-scale map of the City and the City Treasurer acted as Operations Officer.

In the early stages of the war when invasion threatened, an officer of the Norwich Garrison stood by to plot any enemy landings. Another branch of the Civil Defence were the Rest Centres. 13 of these centres were in City day schools and they could, and did, give comfort and sanctuary on more than one occasion to many more than the 2,000 people they were equipped to deal with. In reserve were nine other fully equipped Rest Centres and a further 24 to give emergency refuge. Each Rest Centre had its own billeting officer, a representative of the Assistance Board to issue money for immediate needs, and officials to issue ration books and clothing coupons. The centres were manned by teaching staffs and members of the Women's Voluntary Service.

The fire-watchers or, as they were later called, 'Fireguards' worked unceasingly, often saving complete buildings by their prompt action. Many of these soot-covered Civil Defence workers had reason to be thankful to the various Mobile Canteens whose drivers and helpers shared their hazards, and everybody – civil defence workers, servicemen, and civilians – felt a deep debt of gratitude to the staffs of the Hospitals, the Red Cross, and the St John Ambulance.

Appendix 2

Organization of ARP Wardens

DIVISION 1   *Headquarters II, West Parade*

Group F: Unthank and Eaton
Post F1   Adjoining 3 Trory Street
Post F2   Crook's Place School (Playground)
Post F3   52–62 Cambridge Street
Post F4   151 Newmarket Street
Post F5   Eagle public house, Newmarket Road
Post F6   Christchurch Avenue, Eaton
Post F7   Judges Walk by Unthank Road
Post F8   9 Eaton Hill

Group G: Earlham
Post G1   Clarendon Steps off Clarendon Road
Post G2   Warwick Arms public house, Warwick Street
Post G3   54 Park Lane (early part of war only)
Post G4   Milford Road
Post G5   Enterprise Stores, Muriel Road
Post G6   The Avenues by Christchurch Road
Post G7   Lubbock Close, Elizabeth Fry Road
Post G8   Colman Road

Group H and I: Dereham and Heigham
Post H1   60 West Pottergate
Post H2   Alexandra Tavern, Stafford Street
Post H3   St Thomas Road
Post H4   Heigham Street School
Post H5   By St Barnabas's Church, Russell Street
Post H6   Norwich Corporation Store, Barker Street
Post H7   Nelson Street School
Post H8   City of Norwich Scattered Children's Homes, Turner Road

Group J: Hellesdon and Larkman Lane

Post J1 Gowing's Farm, Hellesdon Hall Road
Post J2 Dereham Road by Larkman Lane
Post J3 Gilbard Road
Post J4 Earlham Grove by Cadge Road
Post J5 Gipsy Lane by Bowthorpe Road

DIVISION 2 *Headquarters III, Milverton Road*

Group C: Thorpe

Post C2 Clarence Road by Carrow Road
Post C3 Rosary Road, Thompsons, Chalk Hill Works
Post C4 Playground, Wolfe Road
Post C5 Lion Wood Road
Post C6 Heathside Road
Post C7 Britannia Road

Group D: Carrow and Lakenham

Post D2 Cricket Ground Road
Post D3 Long John Hill
Post D4 Ber Street Gates
Post D5 Southwell Road by Hall Road

Group E: Tuckswood and Ipswich Road

Post E1 19 St Stephen's Road
Post E4 Sigismund Road by Trafford Road
Post E5 Grove Walk by Cecil Road
Post E6 Fairfield Road near Town Close Road
Post E7 Eaton Road by Waverley Road

Group O: Central

Post O1 5 Bethel Street
Post O2 St Gregory's Alley
Post O3 Three King Lane
Post O4 Thorn Lane
Post O5 Loyalty Court, St Stephen's Street
Post O6 Norwich Lads' Club, King Street
Post O7 Opposite 110 Queen's Road, Victoria Station Coal Yard

DIVISION 3 *Headquarters I, Rackham Road*

Group A: Angel and Woodcock Estate

Post A1 Rackham Road
Post A2 Sun Lane Sunday School, Rosebery Road
Post A3 Middleton Close
Post A4 Woodcock Close
Post A5 Bullard Close
Post A6 Jolly Gardeners public house, Waterloo Road
(this Post later changed to M8)

Group B: New Sprowston and Mousehold

Post B1 George White School, Silver Road
Post B2 128 Barrack Street
Post B3 Sprowston Road by Wall Road
Post B4 Sprowston Road by Gertrude Road
Post B5 Spencer Street
Post B6 Mousehold Avenue Infants' School

Group K: Mile Cross and Drayton

Post K1 Aylsham Road opposite Waterlook Park Avenue
Post K2 Shorncliffe Avenue
Post K3 Drayton Road by Wheeler Road
Post K4 By Norman School, Peterson Road
Post K5 Civic Gardens, Rye Avenue
Post K6 Aylsham Road by Mile Cross Road
Post K7 Wensum Park Gate, St Martin's Road

Group M: The Close and Magdalen Street

Post M1 Tombland
Post M2 St Martin's Palace Plain
Post M3 Charlton Road
Post M4 Bull Close Road Infants' School
Post M5 Sussex Street
Post M6 Duke Street by Colegate
Post M7 Howlett's Court, Botolph Street
Post M8 Heath Road

Appendix 3

Special Constabulary

Division 1 *Headquarters: Park Lane Methodist Chapel*
District 16 Crook's Place
District 18 South Heigham
District 19 South Earlham
District 20 North Heigham
District 21 North Earlham and Hellesdon

Divison 2 *Headquarters: Norwich Lads' Club, King Street*
District 10 Thorpe Hamlet
District 11 Plumstead
District 12 Ber Street and King Street
District 13 Carrow and Thorpe
District 14 New Lakenham
District 15 Old Lakenham
District 17 Eaton

Division 3
District 22 Green Hills and Mill Hill
District 23 Drayton and Mile Cross
District 24 New Catton
District 25 Sprowston and St Clement's Hill

City Divison
District 1 Bethel Street and St Giles Street
District 2 St Stephen's Street
District 3 The Walk and Haymarket
District 4 Prince of Wales Road
District 5 Tombland and The Close
District 6 London Street
District 7 St Benedict's Street
District 8 St Augustine's Sreet
District 9 Magdalen Street

Appendix 4

Auxiliary Fire Service

AFS Filing and Records Office   *12 Lady's Lane*

Auxiliary Firemen (fully trained)
2   Divisional Officers
1   Section Officer
9   Petrol Officers
19   Leading Firemen
188   Firemen
400   Firemen part-time

Havers Road Station
2   large trailer pumps
8   small trailer pumps

Colman's Carrow Works, King Street
1   large trailer pump
6   small trailer pumps

Maudes of Norwich Ltd, Prince of Wales Road
1   motor pump
2   large trailer pumps
5   small trailer pumps

Grange & Samuel, Builders, Mousehold Lane
1   large trailer pump
4   small trailer pumps

Yacht Station
Tangye unit on Police motor-boat

Appendix 5

Rescue Party Depots

Petrol and Oil

60   gallons at Havers Road Station
20   gallons at Sayers Street Station
20   gallons at Tram Sheds Station, Silver Road

Central Station, Bethel Street

3   motor pumps
1   turntable escape
2   small trailer pumps
3   large trailers
3   small trailers
1   Leyland unit on trailer

Norwich Co-operative Society Works Dept, St Stephen's Square

2   large trailer pumps
4   small trailer pumps

Steward & Patteson Ltd, Barrack Street

1   large trailer pump

Cleansing services (Gas)

Tram Sheds, Silver Road
Surrey Street Schools
Sussex Street (reserve)
Lady's Lane (Police and Special Constabulary)

Rescue and Demolition Parties

Corporation Depot, Westwick Street (Headquarters)
Silver Road
Surrey Street
Barker Street (commercial vehicles)
Guardian Road (reserves)

Appendix 6

Sites of Air-Raid Warning Sirens
Centrally controlled

City Hall
City of Norwich School, Eaton Road
Co-operative Dairy, Fiveways
Model Senior Girls' School, Dereham Road
Southall's boot factory, Crome Road
Water-tower, Quebec Road
The Lido dance hall, Aylsham Road
Odeon Theatre, Botolph Street
Co-operative Bakery, Queen's Road

Appendix 7

Balloon Sites

Site 3	Valpy Avenue School playground
Site 8	Municipal school playground, Bowthorpe Road
Site 9	CEYMS Sports Ground, 29 The Avenues
Site 11	School playground between Woodcock Road and Hunter Road
Site 14	Field adjoining Norwich City Stadium, Sprowston Road
Site 15	Raised common land in Valley Drive, Mousehold
Site 16	Ketts Cove entrance of children's playground, Morley Street
Site 17	Cattle-pen, City Station
Site 18	Cricket ground of King Edward VI School, The Close
Site 20	Old greyhound race-track off Thorpe Road
Site 22	Eaton Park off South Park Avenue
Site 23	Grass site south of Newmarket Road, RASC vehicle park
Site 25	Grazing land adjoining Tuckswood Farm at junction of Lakenham Road and Hall Road
Site 28	Chapel Field Gardens Pavilion
Site 29	Pasture land at junction of Fairfield Road, Town Close
Site 31	Lakenham Cricket Ground, City Road
Site 32	Wasteland on bank of the River Wensum adjoining Hardy Road
Site 34	Field opposite Hospital Farm, White Horse Lane, Trowse
Site 36	Crown Point off Whitlingham Lane

Appendix 8

Feeding Centres

Persons whose homes were damaged or who had to be evacuated were directed to:

Lakenham Council School, City Road
Normal School, Dawson Road, Drayton
Bignold School, Crook's Place
Catton Grove School, Catton Grove Road
St Augustine's School, Waterloo Road
Nelson Street School
Mousehold Avenue School
Council Schools, St Leonards Road, Thorpe Hamlet
Council School, Wellesley Avenue
Colman Road School
George White School, Silver Road
Crome and Stuart Schools, Duke Street
Bull Close School
Colman Road Open Air School

Appendix 9

Mobile First-Aid Posts

Open during day
Catton Grove
George White School
Larkman Lane
Long John Hill, Lakenham

Open during blackout
Southall's Sports Club, Rosemary Road
Capitol Cinema, Aylsham Road
The Lido dance hall, Aylsham Road
Ritz Cinema, Dereham Road
Earlham Fiveways public house

Appendix 10

Emergency Water-Tanks (5,000 gallon)

Fruit Market
Tombland by Princes Street
Cattle Market opposite Shirehall
St Catherine's Plain
Golden Ball Street by the Woolpack public house
Victoria Goods Station, St Stephen's Road
Odeon Theatre car park, Botolph Street
Barn Road, opposite Cushions' timber yard
Bethel Street, opposite Rigby's Court
St Saviour's Lane
Theatre Street opposite Lady's Lane
Rear of City Hall
Bowthorpe Road outside Norwich Institution

Appendix 11

Plans for the Evacuation of Norwich

In the event of invasion the following instructions concerning the use of roads radiating from Norwich were to be followed:

Two-way military roads to be kept clear of civilian traffic
North Walsham Road (Constitution Hill)
Sprowston Road
Bracondale (Loddon Road)
Ipswich and New Buckenham Roads
Cromer Road
Earlham Road

One-way military road
Plumstead Road (outwards only)

Roads to be used for civilian evacuees
1   Into Norwich: Thorpe Road and Salhouse Road
2   Out of Norwich: Newmarket Road
3   Earlham Green Lane
4   Two-way roads: Drayton Road and Dereham Road

Civilian refugees on foot would be directed to cross routes and as far as possible across country. These evacuee routes would be:
Route 1
Thorpe Road
Rose Lane
Cattlemarket Street
Golden Ball Street
All Saints' Green
Grove Road, Grove Walk
Cecil Road, Ipswich Road
Lime Tree Road
Newmarket Road to County

Route 2
Thorpe Road
Carrow Road
King Street
Bracondale
Hall Road
Tuckswood Lane
Eaton Road
Newmarket Road
to County

Connecting refugee roads between these two evacuation routes would be:

    (a) Ber Street and Finkelgate
    (b) Southwell Road

Additional refugee routes

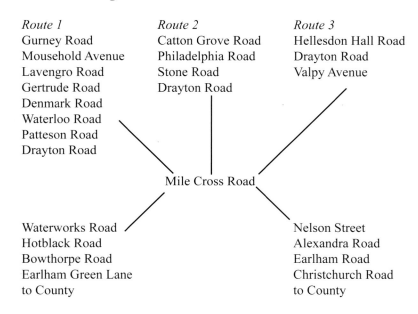

Route 1
Gurney Road
Mousehold Avenue
Lavengro Road
Gertrude Road
Denmark Road
Waterloo Road
Patteson Road
Drayton Road

Route 2
Catton Grove Road
Philadelphia Road
Stone Road
Drayton Road

Route 3
Hellesdon Hall Road
Drayton Road
Valpy Avenue

Mile Cross Road

Waterworks Road
Hotblack Road
Bowthorpe Road
Earlham Green Lane
to County

Nelson Street
Alexandra Road
Earlham Road
Christchurch Road
to County

All roads used by military authorities would be marked:

Up traffic   Black arrow on white background
Down traffic   Black arrow on red ground
Two-way traffic   Both up and down signs used together

Control-points will be manned by members of the Military Police at Boundary Road by Aylsham Road, School Lane by Constitution Hill, Mousehold Lane by Wroxham Road, Plumstead Road by Harvey Lane, Thorpe Road by Harvey Lane, Newmarket Road by Daniels Road, and Earlham Road by Colman Road.

All private cars would be immobilised immediately. Cars still on the roads would be immobilised by the military authorities situated at the exit from Norwich near Eaton, 1 mile south-west of Wymondham, who might contacted by telephone.

Parachutists
Information concerning parachutists would be given to:

1   Britannia Barracks
2   RAF St Faiths
3   Air Ministry, Stoke
4   Regional Police Staff Officer

It is to be noted that owing to the large number of unsubstantiated reports of parachute landings which had reached the Home Security Room, attempts were to be made to obtain some confirmation of such landings before reports were made. All Allied airmen baling out had a small pilot parachute, whereas German parachutists had only a single parachute.

Dep. City Engineer J.W. Taylor
'White Stone'
Colney Lane
Cringleford
Eaton 550

IMPORTANT TELEPHONE NUMBERS

LOCAL:

255558

The Town Clerk	Norwich 1258	
The City Engineer	Thorpe 36	
Mr. J.E. Phillippo	Eaton 703	

Animals in War-time
22129
Mr. H.P. Standley,
13, Red Lion Street — Norwich 709

Report Centre: 20201/6
Earlham Road   Norwich 4061
Market Place   20361 "
(additional numbers Nch.4661)

Urgent Telegrams during Air Raids
Telephone Norwich 6, Extension 12

L. S. E. Traffic Signals
Contact Mr. R.G. Woods,
12, Stratford Drive, City Road,
Telephone - Norwich 3637

Report Centre:

County, Thorpe Road	Norwich 4061	
do. (Mr. Allin)	" 4407	
do. do.		
(9am - 5.30pm)	" 4400	
	120	

Observer Corps
Norwich 2817
or 5398

Ditto. (Alarm Officer)   24891

Chief Gas Identification Officer   2420,
Doctor Corran Business Nch.
Home   Eaton

Home Guard   26942
Drill Hall, Cattlemarket
Colonel Cubitt
Mr. Bassett-Hornor   "18th"

16ᵗʰ Batt
20670
Drill Hall
All Saints Green

Drill Hall
Chapel Field Rd "Batt.
25456

FOREIGN:
Regional Headquarters, Cambridge. "St. Regis", Montague Road, Cambridge.

Police Staff Officer	Cambridge 54037
Fire Brigade Room	" 5041

NOTE: If it is not necessary to speak to the Regional Police Staff Officer, messages should be prefixed with the words, "Police Staff Officer, information only"

The Regional Office may also be contacted on the telephone via Extension 42 on the Police Switchboard (Norfolk Division) and 2 Corps Headquarters.

(If it is not possible to get through to either the Regional Police Staff Officer or the Regional Fire Brigade Headquarters, Cambridge, calls should be made to Newmarket 780 and Regional Headquarters asked for by name and not

16ᵗʰ Batt 16ᵗʰ Batt.
20670 Home 20670

MILITARY TRAFFIC AND EVACUATION

The following instructions concerning the use of roads radiating from Norwich have been issued by the Military Authorities, and will apply should the grave emergency arise:-

Two-way Military Roads to be kept clear of civilian Traffic

North Walsham Road (Constitution Hill)
Sprowston Road
Bracondale (Loddon Road)
Ipswich and New Buckenham Roads
Cromer Road
Earlham Road

One-way Military Road

Plumstead Road (outwards)

Roads for Evacuees

(i) Into Norwich — Thorpe Road and Salhouse Road
(ii) Out of Norwich — Newmarket Road
(iii) Earlham Green Lane
(iv) Two way roads — Drayton Road and Dereham Road

Civilian refugees on foot will be directed to cross routes and, as far as possible, across country

Evacuee Routes

Route No. 1	Route No. 2
Thorpe Road	Thorpe Road
Rose Lane	Carrow Road
Cattlemarket Street	King Street
Golden Ball Street	Bracondale
All Saints Green	Hall Road
Grove Road, Grove Walk	Tuckswood Lane
Cecil Road, Ipswich Road	Eaton Road
Lime Tree Road	Newmarket Road - to County
Newmarket Road — to County	

Connecting refugee roads between these two evacuation routes are -
(a) Ber Street and Finkelgate (b) Southwell Road

Evacuation Roads

Evacuation Roads will not be marked at present. It is intended later to post notices giving instructions to evacuees on these roads.

Appendix 12

Gas Attack

Appendix 13

Places of Worship Damaged or Destroyed

In the event of a gas attack, bleach cream and pails were to be left outside the following chemists:

E R Sayle, 195a Sprowston Road
F Smith, 128 Dereham Road
A J Grand, 2 Alexandra Road
E R Day, 6 St John's Close
Boots Cash Chemists (all branches)
C Benton, 13 White Lion Street
M French, 5 St Stephen's Road
J Cook, 46 St Stephen's Street
Timothy Whites and Taylors, 92 St Benedict's Street
Hurn, 143 Unthank Road
M A Leamon, 68 Prince of Wales Road
L C Hall, 37 Prince of Wales Road
H A King, 38 Exchange Street
D G Hunt, 205 Plumstead Road
L W Parr, 98 Prince of Wales Road
Row & Raylor Ltd, 6 St Stephen's Street
Fuller & Co Ltd, 16–18 Rampant Horse Street
Smith & Sons, 44–48 Magdalen Street
G M Cook, 27 St Augustine's Street
H E De Carle Ltd, 9 St Augustine's Street
J Watson, 43 King Street
A C Brown, 102 Thorpe Road
R Fox, 230 Queen's Road
Norwich Co-operative Society Chemists, 51 St Stephen's Street
C Hurn, 96 and 97 Trinity Street
Jarrold & Sons Ltd, 5 London Street
Norwich Co-operative Socicty, Magdalen Street
B R Veness, 103 St Giles Street
A Larder, 562 Dereham Road
F C Chambers, 74 Magdalen Road

St Anne's, Earlham	Burnt out 27/29 April 1942
St Bartholomew's, Heigham	Gutted by fire 27/29 April 1942
St Benedict's, St Benedict's Street	Almost totally destroyed 27/29 April 1942; tower later restored
St Julian's, St Julian's Alley, King Street	Half destroyed 27 June 1942
St Margaret's, St Benedict's Street	Slight damage 19 October 1942
St Mark's, Hall Road	Slight damage 27 June 1942
St Mary's Baptist Chapel, St Mary's Plain	Gutted 29 April 1942 Further damage 19 October 1942
St Michael-at-Coslany, Oak Street	Roof damage 27 June 1942
St Michael-at-Thorn, Ber Street	Gutted by fire 27 June 1942
St Paul's, St Paul's Square	Gutted by fire 27 June 1942
St Peter Mancroft, St Peter's Street	Slight damage to masonry 27/29 April 1942
St Stephen's, Rampant Horse Street	Slight damage 29 April 1942
St Swithin's, St Benedict's Street	Slight damage 19 October 1942
St Thomas's, Earlham Road	Gutted by fire 29 April 1942
Cathedral Church of the Holy and Undivided Trinity	Transept roof damaged 27 June 1942
Baptist Church, Dereham Road	Badly damaged 27/29 April 1942
Friends' Meeting House, Upper Goat Lane	Seriously damaged 29 April 1942
Jewish Synagogue	Gutted by fire 27 June 1942

Appendix 14

Public Houses Damaged and Destroyed

Albert Stores, 1 Russell Street	Damaged 27/29.4.42
Albert Tavern, 57 Devonshire Street Rear	Demolished 18.3.43
Alexandra, 148 Old Palace Road	Damaged 27/29.4.42
Alma Tavern, 92 Pottergate	Damaged 27/29.4.42
Anchor, Rising Sun Lane	Damaged 27.5.42
Anchor of Hope, 114 Oak Street	Destroyed 27/29.4.42
Bakers' Arms, 213 Heigham Street	Damaged 27/29.4.42
Barn Tavern, 1 Dereham Road	Badly damaged 27/29.4.42
Bartholomew Tavern, 27 Thorn Lane	Damaged 27/29.4.42
Belle Vue Tavern, 46 St Philip's Road	Damaged 27/29.4.42
Black Boys, 30 Colegate	Damaged 27.4.42
Black Eagle, 20 Rupert Street	Damaged 27/29.4.42
Black Horse, 115 Heigham Street	Damaged 27/29.4.42
Black Horse Inn, 23 St Giles Street	Damaged 27/29.4.42
Boar's Head, 2 Surrey Street	Severely Damaged 27/29.4.42
Canterbury Tavern, 54 Napier Street	Damaged 27/29.4.42
Cardinal's Cap, 86 St Benedict's Street	Destroyed 27/29.4.42
Carpenters' Arms, 33 Thorn Lane	Damaged 27/29.4.42
Cock, 151 Adelaide Street	Damaged 27/29.4.42
Crawshay Arms, 151 Philadelphia Lane	Damaged 27/29.4.42
Constitution Tavern, 140 Constitution Hill	Damaged 27/29.4.42
Crown, 71 St Benedict's Street	Damaged 27/29.4.42
Crown and Angel, 41 St Stephen's Street	Severely damaged 27/29.4.42
Curriers' Arms, 114 Essex Street	Destroyed 27/29.4.42
Cygnet, 147 Churchill Road	Damaged 27/29.4.42
Denmark Arms, 43 Sandringham Road	Damaged 27/29.4.42
Derby Arms, 75 Derby Street	Destroyed 27/29.4.42
Dial, 131 Dereham Road	Destroyed 27/29.4.42
Distillery, 48 Dereham Road	Severely Damaged 27/29.4.42
Dolphin Inn, 252 Heigham Street	Gutted by fire 27/29.4.42
Duke of Connaught, 60 Livingstone Street	Destroyed 27/29.4.42
Duke of Connaught, 72 Prince of Wales Rd	Damaged 27/29.4.42
Duke of Wellington, 5 Chapel Street	Damaged 27/29.4.42
Duke of York, 21 Bishop Bridge Road	Damaged 27/29.4.42
Dun Cow, 167 Oak Street	Damaged 27/29.4.42
Dyers' Arms, Magdalen Road	Damaged 27/29.4.42
Earl of Cardigan, 56 Orchard Street	Damaged 27/29.4.42
Earl of Leicester, Dereham Road	Damaged 27/29.4.42
Elephant and Castle, 120 King Street	Damaged 27.5.42
Elm Tavern, 118 Magdalen Road	Damaged 27/29.4.42
Engineers' Tavern, 17 St Julian Street	Damaged 27.5.42
Essex Tavern, 67 Rupert Street	Damaged 27/29.4.42
Evening Gun, 7 Rosary Road	Badly damaged 27/29.4.42
Fellmongers' Arms, Oak Street	Destroyed 1942
Flower in Hand, 20 Pitt Street	Damaged 27/29.4.42
Foundry Bridge Tavern, Mountergate	Damaged 27/29.4.42
Fountain, 89 St Benedict's Street	Destroyed 27/29.4.42
Free Trade Inn, 35 St Peter's Street	Damaged 27/29.4.42
Gardeners' Arms, 4 Timber Hill	Damaged 27/29.4.42
Gatehouse, Dereham Road	Damaged 27/29.4.42
George IV, 72 Ber Street	Damaged 27/29.4.42
George IV, 187 Essex Street	Damaged 27/29.4.42
Golden Lion, 15 St John Maddermarket	Damaged 2.8.42
Green Hills, 12 Green Hill Road	Damaged 27/29.4.42
Greyhound, 1 Greyhound Opening	Damaged 27/29.4.42
Horse Barracks, 173 Barrack Street	Severely damaged 27/29.4.42
Horse Shoes, 21 Palace Street	Damaged 27/29.4.42
Ipswich Tavern, 4 St Stephen's Plain	Damaged 27/29.4.42
Jolly Farmers' Inn, 5 Farmers Avenue	Burnt Out 27.5.42
Jolly Gardeners, 138 Waterloo Road	Damaged 27/29.4.42
Jolly Maltsters, 255 King Street	Damaged 27.5.42
Kett's Castle, 29 Ketts Hill	Damaged 27/29.4.42
Key and Castle, 150 Oak Street	Damaged 27/29.4.42
King Edward VII, Aylsham Road	Damaged 27/29.4.42
King's Arms, 1 Rosary Road	Damaged 27/29.4.42
King's Arms, 38 Botolph Street	Damaged 27/29.4.42
King's Arms, 8 Ber Street	Damaged 27.5.42
Lord John Russell, 66 Dereham Road	Damaged 27/29.4.42
Lord Nelson, 286 Dereham Road	Damaged 27/29.4.42
Lord Nelson, Nelson Street	Damaged 27/29.4.42
Lord Raglan, 30 Bishop Bridge Road	Severely damaged 27/29.4.42

Mancroft Arms, 39 Mancroft Street	Damaged 27/29.4.42
Manor House, Drayton Road	Damaged 27/29.4.42
Marlborough Arms, 43 Spencer Street	Damaged 27/29.4.42
Marquis of Lothian, 42 Lothian Street	Damaged 27/29.4.42
Morrison Lodge, Harvey Lane	Damaged 27/29.4.42
New City, 70 Shadwell Street, Crooks Place	Damaged 27/29.4.42
Norfolk Tavern, 27 Norfolk Street	Severely damaged 27/29.4.42
Norfolk Tavern, 62 Rupert Street	Damaged 27/29.4.42
Oak Shades, Lower Goat Lane	Damaged 27/29.4.42
Old Barge Inn, 123 King Street	Damaged 27/29.4.42
Orchard Tavern, 36 Heigham Street	Damaged 27/29.4.42
Orchard Tavern, 38 Mountergate	Severely damaged 2.12.40
Park House, Catton Grove Road	Damaged 27/29.4.42
Paul Pry, 45 Grapes Hill	Damaged 27/29.4.42
Perseverance, 35–37 Adelaide Street	Damaged 27/29.4.42
Pheasant Cock, 244 Queen's Road	Damaged 27/29.4.42
Plough, 58 St Benedict's Street	Damaged 27/29.4.42
Prince of Wales, 8 Prince of Wales Road	Damaged 27/29.4.42
Prince of Wales, 34 St Benedict's Street	Damaged 19.10.42
Prospect House, 93 Aylsham Road	Damaged 27/29.4.42
Provision Stores, 107 Dereham Road	Damaged 27/29.4.42
Queen Adelaide, 57 Pitt Street	Badly damaged 27/29.4.42 Skittle alley used as pub for many years
Queen Victoria, 111 Adelaide Street	Damaged 27/29.4.42
Rainbow, 56 Old Palace Road	Severely damaged 27/29.4.42
Raven, 1 St Giles Street	Severely damaged 27/29.4.42
Red Lion, 79 Bishopgate	Damaged 27/29.4.42
Reindeer, 10 Dereham Road	Damaged 27/29.4.42
Rifleman, Cross Lane	Damaged 27/29.4.42, 5.9.42
Robin Hood, 106–108 Dereham Road	Damaged 27/29.4.42
Roebuck, 47 Southwell Road	Damaged 27/29.4.42
Royal Oak, 221–223 Essex Street	Damaged 27/29.4.42
Royal Oak, 132 Oak Street	Damaged 27/29.4.42
St Giles Gate Stores, 100 St Giles Street	Damaged 27/29.4.42
Sandringham Arms, 50 William Street	Damaged 27/29.4.42
Shakespeare, 19 Theatre Street	Damaged 27/29.4.42
Shirehall, 25 Cattle Market Street	Damaged 27/29.4.42
Somerleyton Tavern, 58 Somerleyton Street	Destroyed 27/29.4.42
Spear in Hand, 27 Vauxhall Street	Destroyed 27.5.42
Sportsman, 83–85 Northumberland Street	Severely damaged 27/29.4.42
Spread Eagle, 35 Sussex Street	Damaged 27/29.4.42
Staff of Life, 72 Augustine's Street	Damaged 27/29.4.42
Stafford Arms, 35 Heigham Road	Damaged 27/29.4.42
Stag, 65 At Benedict's Street	Badly damaged 27/29.4.42
Standley Arms, 33 Magdalen Street	Damaged 27/29.4.42
Surrey Inn, 74 Grove Road	Severely damaged 27/29.4.42
Swiss Cottage, 16 Dereham Road	Damaged 27/29.4.42
Thorn Tavern, 25 Ber Street	Damaged 27.5.42
Three Kings, 46 St Benedict's Street	Damaged 27/29.4.42
Trafford Arms, 61 Grove Road	Severely damaged 27.5.42
Trumpet, 72 St Stephens Street	Damaged 27/29.4.42
Tuns, 2 All Saints' Green	Damaged 27/29.4.42
Tuns, 2 Unthank Road	Damaged 27/29.4.42
Unicorn Inn, 28 St Stephen's Street	Severely damaged 27/29.4.42
Vauxhall, 47 Vauxhall Street	Destroyed 18.2.41
Victory, 47 Dereham Road	Damaged 27/29.4.42
Vine, 2 St Benedict's Street	Damaged 19.10.42
Waterworks Tavern, 253 Northumberland Street	Damaged 27/29.4.42
West End Retreat, 1 Browne Street	Damaged 27/29.4.42
West Pottergate Stores, 34 West Pottergate	Damaged 27/29.4.42
Whip and Nag, 3 Pitt Street	Damaged 27/29.4.42
White Hart, 6 Ber Street	Damaged 27.5.42
White Lion, 73 Oak Street	Damaged 27/29.4.42
White Lion, 73 St Benedict's Street	Severely damaged 27/29.4.42
Windmill, 24 Ber Street	Damaged 27.5.42
Windsor Castle, 68 Barrack Street	Damaged 2.8.42
Wine Coopers' Arms, 13 Distillery Street	Damaged 27/29.4.42
Woodcock, Woodcock Road	Damaged 27/29.4.42
Yarn Factory Tavern, 153 Colegate	Damaged 5.9.42

Index

This select index includes street names, organisations, major buildings and businesses in the main text. It does not cover lists within the main text, or the appendices.